THE
ADVENTURE
BEGINS

A PRACTICAL GUIDE TO
EXPLORING THE BIBLE WITH UNDER-12s

T E R R Y   C L U T T E R H A M

Scripture Union

Scripture Union, 207–209 Queensway, Bletchley, Milton Keynes, MK2 2EB, England.

First published 1996

ISBN 0 86201 906 0

British Library Cataloguing–in–Publication Data
A catalogue record for this book is available from the British Library.

Cover design and illustration by Ross Advertising and Design Limited.

Phototypeset by Intype London Ltd.
Printed and bound in Great Britain by Cox & Wyman Ltd, Reading.

For Sue, Lucy and Anna,
three Bible explorers
who have helped me find the way

∾ CONTENTS ∾

∽ SOWERS OF SEEDS ∾

In 1992, I wrote a Scripture Union report called 'Children and the Bible', consisting of many stimulating conversations with people who were passionate about helping children to listen to God through the Bible. This book has grown out of that report.

I am particularly grateful to Francis Bridger, Ron Buckland, Margaret Cooling, Glenn Cupitt, David V Day, Martin Dowson, John W Drane, Ron Fountain, David Gamble, Helen Martin, John Goldingay, Eric Gower, Philip Juler, Harold Kallemeyn, Steve Pearce, John Tigwell, Pat Travis and Terry Williams. They may recognise as 'seedlings' in this book some of the 'seeds' they sowed back then. Other contributors to the report will have sown seeds that I am not able to point to so precisely, but I owe them much too.

By their careful reading of this book, Vernon Blackmore, Penny Frank and Rory Keegan have been a huge encouragement to me.

Of course, there would simply be no book without the many children and young people with whom I have had the privilege of exploring the Bible. They have kept me in touch with reality, often helping me to see what I have missed and enthusing me to carry on exploring for myself. I owe them most of all.

Terry Clutterham

❧ ACKNOWLEDGEMENTS ❧

Page 14: East 17, 'Hold My Body Tight'. Written by Anthony Mortimer, Matthew Rowbottom and Richard Stannard, © 1994 Porky Publishing/Polygram Music Publishing Limited. Lyrics reproduced by kind permission of the publisher.

Page 16: Brian James, 'The Moral Curriculum', *The Mail on Sunday*, 20 June 1993, © SOLO Syndication Limited.

Page 18: *The Message* by Eugene H Peterson, © 1993, 1994, 1995, NavPress Publishing Group.

Page 25: John Hull, *God-Talk With Young Children*, Birmingham Papers in Religious Education No 2, The University of Birmingham and the Christian Education Movement 1990.

Page 49: J C Pollock, *The Good Seed*, Hodder & Stoughton.

Page 57: Linette Martin, 'Children Fed on Straw', *Third Way*.

Page 83: Annie Dillard, *Pilgrim at Tinker Creek*, Harper & Row (HarperCollins Publishers Limited).

Page 92: Taken from *How to Read The Bible as Literature* by Leland Ryken, © 1984 by the Zondervan Corporation. Used by permission of Zondervan Publishing House.

Pages 94–96: Jeffrey Archer, *A Twist in the Tale*, Hodder & Stoughton; 'My Grandad's Old' from *Startling Verse for All the Family* by Spike Milligan (Michael Joseph, 1987), p49, copyright © Spike Milligan Productions 1987, reproduced by permission of Penguin Books Limited; HRH The Prince of Wales, article in *The National Trust Magazine*, Autumn 1995; Terry Waite, *Taken on Trust*, Hodder & Stoughton, 1993, reproduced by permission of Hodder & Stoughton Limited; Terry Pratchett, *Truckers*, © Terry Pratchett 1989, published by Transworld Publishers Limited. All rights reserved.

Pages 117 and 120: Lawrence O Richards, *Talkable Bible Stories*, Fleming H Revell, a division of Baker Book House Company, Grand Rapids, Michigan, © 1983, 1991.

Page 118: J R R Tolkien, *Tree and Leaf*, Unwin Paperbacks.

Page 121: Robert Coles, *The Spiritual Life of Children*, HarperCollins*Religious*, an imprint of HarperCollins*Publishers* Limited.

Page 138: Dietrich Bonhoeffer, *Life Together*, © SCM Press 1954.

Page 139: Taken from the revised edition of *Work and Worship* by Ben Patterson © 1994, published by InterVarsity Press, Leicester.

❧ SHOOTS ❧

GOD ON EVERY PAGE

Lucy, aged four, suddenly ran to fetch her Bible. I thought
we were having a pretty good time reading *Mr Fussy*, but
clearly not good enough! She thrust the Bible under my
nose and burst out, 'I love the Bible – for keeping places in
and for giving us songs to sing in church. And it tells us
about Jesus.' I was really excited because she wasn't just
repeating what she had heard me say. I would never have
thought of being pleased about the Bible being good for
'keeping places in' and for 'giving us songs to sing in church'!
Here was a book she was growing to love.

Another time when she was 'reading' her Bible, I asked
her what she was doing. 'I'm looking for God on every
page,' she replied, as if I should have known. A moment of
pure, unexpected joy for me – such spiritual insight in one
so young! But what I had first understood by her answer
didn't quite match up with what she actually meant. She had
just started learning to read, and the combination of letters
G-O-D was hugely fascinating to her. So she was scouring
the pages, pointing to them each time they occurred. I
smiled because, even if her comment wasn't what I first
thought, she knew that the Bible was for her and that somehow she could find God in its pages.

WHY THIS BOOK?

Children of all ages – and adults too, of course! – have the
capacity to love the Bible and to hear God speaking powerfully to them through it. But 'trees by a stream', as Psalm 1
calls those who are nourished by God's word, will need
our careful help if they are to discover and maintain their
enthusiasm for the Bible through the years.

I hope this book will be of practical use to those of us

who see ourselves as apprehensive troubleshooters rather than confident high-fliers when we explore the Bible with our own children or with those in the group we lead. (Throughout the book, 'your children' or 'our children' can be taken to mean either.) We must be true to the Bible and realistic about what children themselves are like and can do. Sounds a bit of a tall order? We must aim high, because when we open the Bible with children we shall be helping them to 'see' God himself and what he wants them to know.

However, God doesn't say that we have to be successful in our task — 'success' is the Holy Spirit's business. God asks no more of us then our best *attempt* to be faithful to both the Bible and to our children. I want this book to encourage us in our 'best attempt'.

WHAT ARE WE AIMING TO DO?

Faith in God changes with time. This change may be growth or decay, a deepening of faith or a falling away from God. Whether we consider our children 'Christians' or not, we must explore the Bible with them in a way that will help them keep on saying 'Yes' to God.

By seeing God clearly at work through the Bible, by following the example of those they see living its message, and by wanting to be part of all that God is doing through Christ, children of Christian parents will, we hope, come to own the faith for themselves. This 'owning' may be the big 'Yes' to God we usually call conversion; but it need not always be such an earth-shattering event. Essentially, it is one more very significant step along the road — children recognising that 'this' Lord, and 'our' Lord, wants to be 'their' Lord, and asking Christ into their lives for ever.

Our Bible exploration with children who have no Christian background will aim to help them reach the point where they own the faith they see modelled in us, and will encourage them to keep growing in it.

We don't have to categorise children as 'Christians' or 'non-Christians' before we decide how to explore the Bible with them. As long as we use the Bible with integrity and treat children with respect, God will take care of both the nurture of Christian children and the progress towards faith and new life of non-Christian children. Both can be called 'growth'.

HOW DOES IT WORK?

Since we cannot help children with something we know nothing about or don't find exciting ourselves, chapters one and two of this book are aimed at helping us grasp the vision and get more out of the Bible ourselves.

The titles of chapters three to nine all reflect statements children sometimes make about the Bible. Their comments show us some of the problems that need to be overcome. These chapters all follow the same basic pattern. First, we get to the 'Root problem' by seeing how each difficulty with the Bible is expressed in children's lives. Then, in 'Growing trees', we examine how we can best help children overcome this difficulty. Finally, the 'Plans for growth' sections offer practical tips to help us identify the difficulty and take in what the chapter has been about.

I suggest that if our children are to listen to God and keep on wanting to listen to him through the Bible, they need to:

Know what the Bible is and how important it is (chapter one).

Have the help of an enthusiastic adult (chapters two and three).

Anticipate Bible exploration as an adventure in which they will come face to face with God (chapter four).

Know that their own understanding of the Bible has been acknowledged and valued (chapter five).

Develop their own natural explorer's skills with the different kinds of writing in the Bible, and be taught new skills (chapters six and seven).

Learn to reflect on their own life stories with the help of Bible stories (chapter eight).

Begin to appreciate the Bible as the one big story of God's plan to create and save his people (chapter nine).

Respond to the discoveries they make within the Bible's pages, and therefore grow (chapter eleven.)

Chapter ten provides Bible activity ideas to use with children, to help overcome the difficulties.

THE ADVENTURE BEGINS

When we realise that God is on every page of the Bible, our adventure begins. We have something vital to discover about him in every part of his word. When our children realise this too, together we become a team of explorers.

Delving into the Bible with children will mean living adventurously. Not only shall we attempt thinking, attitudes and activities that we have never tried before, but our children themselves will be giving us as much as we give them: perhaps they will bring us fresh insights and thrilling new ways of getting 'under the skin' of the Bible.

We mustn't fear the adventure. The Holy Spirit is committed to helping children know Christ and hear God clearly – much more than we could ever be. We will do what we can to help our children with the Bible in the best possible way, but thank God that the Holy Spirit takes the responsibility for the lasting effects of our adventure together.

Chapter One

TREES BY A STREAM

'I will bless those
who put their trust in me.
They are like trees growing near a stream
and sending out roots to the water.
They are not afraid when hot weather comes,
because their leaves stay green;
They have no worries when there is no rain;
they keep on bearing fruit.'
(Jeremiah 17:7–8.)

OFF THE TOURIST TRACK

Edinburgh, St Anne's-on-Sea, Bedgebury, Uttoxeter . . .
What the tourist books don't bother to tell us is that near
all these places there are trees growing by streams. I know. I
have sat in the shade of them, surrounded by crowds of
children. And the trees have been the very centre of
attention.

We can learn a lot from trees. Once, as part of a residential
holiday activity programme, our team of twenty adults and
fifty children took a bus trip to see a tree that was by a
stream. Crazy? The bus driver certainly thought so. Off went
our double-decker to – yes – a load of trees in the middle
of nowhere! Of course it was crazy. But being where biblical
images are happening can be a very powerful experience.
The image of those trees remains firmly fixed in my memory
and, I hope, in the children's memories too.

One boy tried to push over a massive willow, then two girls
lent a hand. Ten, twelve, twenty, forty, fifty of us strained.
Completely silly – and hopeless! Everyone fell about laugh-
ing. This tree wasn't budging. On our way back to sit down,
we stumbled over the gnarled roots that were fighting for
space in the earth, but which all ended up reaching out into
the water. Amazing! We lay back and looked up at the sky

through the shiny, wiggly, willow leaves. Somehow, enjoying trees doesn't seem so silly in a crowd.

In spite of the storms and hurricanes tearing at the countryside over the previous years, and the hot, dry summers scorching the grass on the bank of the stream, this tree was still standing firm and fresh, doing exactly what a tree is supposed to do — whatever that is.

Afterwards, I encouraged all those children to have a tree planted in their name, if they wanted to. Why? So that in the next millennium, all over the country, many sturdy trees would sway in the wind as symbols of the determination of those children to be nourished by God's word.

DIFFERENT WORLDS

Back in Bible times, Joab sat on the dusty floor of the synagogue, at the feet of his rabbi. There in front of the rabbi, on a low table, were the scrolls of Scripture. At school Joab learnt to read and, of course, to recite the Law of the Lord. He heard stories and he memorised poems that encapsulated teaching from the Law: he repeated, he chanted, he learnt the Law by acrostics until it was thoroughly fixed in his mind. He began with the Shema, the command to love God: 'Israel, remember this! The Lord — and the Lord alone — is our God. Love the Lord your God with all your heart, with all your soul, and with all your strength' (Deuteronomy 6:4–5). Then he moved on to the Hallel, a psalm of praise (like Psalm 135) that would be used at the great festivals. Next, he would learn the story of the Creation and the laws about offerings and sacrifices.

However, the Law was much more than simply words that flowed through his mind: like a deep underground stream, it wound its way through the whole of Jewish culture. Wherever Joab turned, there were reminders of the demands of the Law and of the goodness of God — in the synagogue, in tephillim boxes worn on wrists, in phylacteries strapped around foreheads, in the mezuzah box on the doorpost of his house and in the home itself. Eventually he would become a 'son of the Law', when he was thirteen, at the celebration of his bar mitzvah.

The 'waters' of the Law would always be there. Joab's roots would be firmly fixed in it and he would drink very deeply. Not that he was perfect, but he certainly knew the facts and the benefits of how God intended him to live.

For late twentieth-century, gentile children, the world is very different to Joab's, though they are still in desperate need of hearing from God. Many of the messages they constantly 'drink in' at home, at school and in the street, are certainly not God's word, though there are 'good' messages too. Let's take a brisk walk through their world with our eyes open and see the mix of 'good' and 'not good' . . .

Get into Pitfighter! The story: kick in lots of people. Starring: three clean-cut, muscly hulks and loads of dodgy perv-mongers with masks. (Review of a video game.)

Adopt a humpback whale and give these gentle giants a gift of life . . . Help us to help them live a natural life, to evolve and exist as nature meant without the perils and dangers so often encountered. (Advertisement from the International Wildlife Coalition Trust, in *Live and Kicking*.)

Search for the hero inside yourself
Until you find the key to your life.
  (From a song by The Young People.)

'Where would you really like to be right now?'
'At a hard-core rave with a nice girl. Or in bed with a nice bird at a posh hotel and having sex, and then go to sleep. Mind you, I haven't got the money for a posh hotel yet, so it'll have to be at home. Ha ha.'
(Interview with a pop star in *Smash Hits*, a magazine read by twelve-year-olds.)

So come on and put them arms around me,
Hold me real close,
  like an aura surround me.
I need to feel ya body,
The warmth of ya skin.
I need to know the beauty
  and the secret within.
And while another would be penetrating,
I'll still be stimulating,
Contemplating on a vision vibrating,
  Waiting with the key

To set your feelings free.
Watcha gonna do for me?
(From 'Hold My Body Tight' by East 17.)

Meanwhile over at the 'innocent' comic shelf . . .

Girl: Ooh! What crazy pet have you got now?
Boy: It's a Chinese porcupine! Don't worry! It's perfectly tame!
Evil Eye thinks (*as an eye that watches everything*): A tame
porcupine? How pointless! Come on, Spiky! Use those quills to
get some thrills! (*The Evil Influence zaps the porcupine.*)
Porcupine: Heh! So they think I'm tame, do they?
(From comic cartoon called 'Evil Eye', in *Whizzer and Chips
Holiday Special*, Summer 1995.)

No matter what anyone tells you, it's not OK to 'just try' a
drug once or twice. Once is enough to kill you. How do you
know how your body will react? Or even if it is what the pusher
says it is? . . . Sniffing aerosols or glue can kill too – they can
make you suffocate. (From 'The Growing-Up Guide' in *Shout*
magazine, © D C Thomson & Co Ltd.)

Do your cards know something you don't? Call the Tarot Line
to discover the secrets of your future success. Learn what the
tarot cards have to say about everything that affects your future
in money and love. Uncover the truth! Discover the future!

Libra. YOU: If you've been having little or no success when
it comes to someone you fancy, that's all set to change. After
April 22, there ain't no stopping you! YOUR FRIENDS: If
you've had minor tiff with a mate, this fortnight is a good
time to kiss and make up. NUMBER: 6. COLOUR: Navy
blue. DAY: Saturday 24.

Some of the media messages are:

'Any sex is OK as long as it's safe and between two consenting
adults.'
'Fit is in!'
'Save the nice things of the world.'
'Look good and sexy, not fat!'
'There's a spiritual world out there – somewhere.'
'Everyone's doing it – whatever it is! But don't do it if it's
dangerous.'
'You can escape – for a while.'
'Independent is cool.'
'Gossip is juicy.'

'Do yourself justice.'
'Don't get mad – get even!'

If we take time to immerse ourselves in some of the material our children are hearing, watching, reading and playing, we will soon pick up what the subtle and not-so-subtle 'voices' are telling them. Plan 1 in 'Plans for Growth' (page 33) gives hints on how we can do this.

Hardly a week passes without Britain agonising over some fresh example of society's lack of moral judgment and, more worryingly, without leaders, doctors and lawyers saying, 'Declaring what is right and wrong is not our role.' This chasm has been swallowing up our young. Talk to social workers, police, court officials, and they will insist that their greatest burden is not the defiance of those children who steal and vandalise, the contempt of those caught car stealing and granny beating, but the bleak evidence that so many have no grasp of the very concept of right and wrong. (From an article called 'The Moral Curriculum' by Brian James, in *The Mail on Sunday*, 20 June 1993.)

We are living in what has been called the 'post-modern' era, a climate of bewildering patterns of thought, morals and lifestyles which surround and influence our children as well as teenagers and adults. Yet many aspects of post-modernism sound promising for the Bible.

• There is a ground swell of nostalgia for the past. Promising for the Bible which is stuffed full of history and old ways? No, any past will do, and pagan pasts seem more attractive.

• There is respect for all traditions and shades of opinion. Promising for the Bible which stands for 'traditional' values? No, if there is something good in *everything*, there is nothing distinctively good in *anything*, and something that claims to lead to *all* truth seems unacceptably arrogant or at least short-sighted.

• There is the illusion of maximum choice and power being put into the hands of every child, teenager and adult. Videos enable us to watch what we want when we want. Computers allow us to shape, edit and distort reality. We can't believe that anything is really what it appears – any real-life image can be manipulated. Promising for the Bible which is 'fixed' beyond our tampering? No, if children can't control it, they're not that interested.

● There is a belief in what works, not in what is real. Promising for the Bible which is full of truth that 'works'? No, when something works, it has to work pretty instantly and give its user a 'buzz'. The Bible doesn't – it requires a long-term commitment to it.

So how can the Bible become the life-giving stream for children who are buffeted by these winds or scorched by these rays? In an 'instant', 'take it or leave it', 'be your own hero', entertainment-oriented culture, how can we help children to explore a black-print book that involves hard work if they are to get the best out of it? How will they ever grow to love a book which, in the popular view, is either largely fictional or else will only tell them in the end that they aren't anyone's hero and that they have failed? It doesn't seem like a life-giving stream at all – more like a drain. This is the struggle we are engaged in, but we mustn't give up. As we have already discovered, we are aiming breathtakingly high. We have to. Lives are at stake.

Children are fragile yet resilient. They are easily influenced yet often stubbornly self-willed. They are vulnerable yet skilful at making the rest of the world revolve around them. (We adults are too, but less innocently and we conceal it better!) Because life is precariously balanced for children, we want them to hear 'voices' that will tell them the truth in ways appropriate to their age – not skew their view of themselves, the world, God and everything, and make them children of despair. Early impressions stick.

Teach a child how he should live, and he will remember it all his life. (*Proverbs 22:6*.)

WHY BOTHER WITH THE BIBLE?

We know that the best voice for children to listen to is God's. He has the right view of everything. No other voice is totally reliable. We long for children to love and respond to the Bible, because we know that, through it, they can hear the one who doesn't use his powerful words to browbeat them but to speak the truth and invite a positive response.

Jesus criticised the Pharisees because they used the Scriptures to place intolerable burdens on other people's lives. They failed to see how God's word pointed to him and thus to freedom:

> You have your heads in your Bibles constantly because you think you'll find eternal life there. But you miss the forest for the trees. These Scriptures are all about me! And here I am, standing right before you, and you aren't willing to receive from me the life you say you want. (John 5:39–40, from *The Message* by Eugene H Peterson.)

We and our children need to bother with the Bible because in it we come face to face with God and are invited to know Christ for ourselves. This encounter can shape our lives in a way that pleases God and contributes towards the vast plan he has for all creation.

Whole lives lived God's way

> How can young people keep their lives pure?
>   By obeying your commands.
> With all my heart I try to serve you;
>   keep me from disobeying your commandments.
> I keep your law in my heart,
>   so that I will not sin against you.
> I praise you, O Lord;
>   teach me your ways.
> I will repeat aloud
>   all the laws you have given.
> I delight in following your commands
>   more than in having great wealth.
> I study your instructions;
>   I examine your teachings.
> I take pleasure in your laws;
>   your commands I will not forget.
>
>   (*Psalm 119:9–16*.)

We all have the capacity to think, feel and act, with wills that can be for or against God. In these verses from Psalm 119, the writers talks passionately about how God's 'laws', 'commands', 'instructions' and 'teachings' have changed his thinking, feelings and actions, thus shaping his whole life for God. Do you see how all three aspects appear in what he says? For example, he has 'studied' (thought hard about) God's instructions, he 'delights' (finds great joy) in obeying them, and expects them to shape his 'ways' (actions).

The Bible is the story of how God gives himself totally to create, shape, save and make his people whole again. Every time we open the Bible, God invites us to meet him and to love him. It is as if he says, 'Look, here I am. This is a picture of my total commitment to you. Now, in response, I want you to be totally committed to me – heart, soul, mind and strength. I'm looking for as much love as you can give me, as much faith as you can put in me.'

Now if we ask anyone what faith is, their answers will probably touch on one or more of three concepts – 'understanding the faith', 'having faith' or 'stepping out in faith'. The kind of faith God looks for involves our thinking and belief (understanding the faith), our emotional trust in God (having faith), and our practical action (stepping out in faith, or godly actions). In Mark 12:28–30, Jesus says that loving God involves our 'hearts' (our inner being, personalities or wills), our 'souls' (emotions), our 'minds' (thinking power) and our 'strength' (physical abilities and actions). God wants all that we are to be directed towards him, pleasing to him and glorifying of him. He wants to shape the whole of us so that we become perfect. Only his word shows us clearly how he wants to change us. His is the powerful voice that invites children – and adults – without pressure, to reach their full potential in him.

Plans 2 and 3 in 'Plans for Growth' (pages 33–34) will help you to see how children can be totally engrossed in and profoundly influenced by what they hear.

We want children to know the authority of the Bible

Authority creates or demands a response. Because the Bible is truth from the Source of all truth, we can safely allow it to impact on us and our children in any way that God wants. Indeed, we want to encourage children to grow into adults who encounter the Bible not with a critical frame of mind, as if they know best and the Bible might be wrong, but as vulnerable people who know they need to be changed by what God says to them through it.

Children, however, may not need to make a conscious effort to be vulnerable to the Bible. Because they are naturally more impressionable, they will probably be more open to the Bible's impact anyway, more awestruck by what they see of God within its pages.

Recognising the authority of the Bible will always mean much more than the word 'obedience' suggests, because the Bible isn't the rule-book we have often said it is. For instance, how do we 'obey' the opening chapter of Genesis, or a psalm which is an honest prayer to God, or the vision of Revelation? Each part of the Bible demands its own type of response (as we shall see in chapter seven), and adults are under the Bible's authority when they ask, 'What kind of response does this passage ask of us?' Children may well experience the authoritative impact of the Bible and the revelation of God contained in it without having consciously to ask this question.

Through the Bible, God may want to disturb us, comfort us, humble us, make us less sinful, encourage us, give us hope, guide our decisions, make us squeal with delight or gasp with wonder, or help us to love him more in another way. God's word can change our thinking, feelings, actions and wills. To let God change us in any of these ways through what we read or hear in the Bible is to recognise its authority. In the end, we are not talking about the authority of a book, but the authority of God.

So children need to bother with the Bible because it builds all aspects of faith as they respond to its authority. It can shape their beliefs, direct their emotions and inspire their actions towards God, as the stream nourishes and strengthens the tree standing beside it.

> Bible Activity 1 'What's the Difference?' (page 141) will help us talk with our children about what makes the Bible unlike anything else we read, and much more important.

The Bible shapes their beliefs

Children find themselves in a 'supermarket' of beliefs, exposed to the influences of many different religions and values. They may choose the belief that excites them from one shelf, add to it one that fascinates them from another shelf, one that makes them feel valued from another shelf, and one their parents have taught them from yet another.

Let's eavesdrop on a real–life conversation between an adult and a six-year-old, recorded for a BBC documentary on childhood:

Adult: What happens to a gerbil when it dies?
Child: I don't really know. I think they go up to Gerbil Heaven.
A: There is one, is there? There's a gerbil heaven?
C: Yes. I've been to Gerbil Land. I've been to Animal Land where animals can talk, where animals can stand on their back legs, where animals can shop . . .
A: Really?
C: Where animals live in houses . . . in stables.
A: Do you think that we die like a gerbil dies?
C: Well, I don't really think so because we can't get buried under a stone, under this wincy little stone. It was the size of a gerbil, that stone was.
A: But you think we do die, though? Not like a gerbil, but we would die perhaps?
C: Yes.
A: Where do we go when we die?
C: We go to Human Being Heaven.
A: Human Being Heaven. Who do we meet there?
C: We meet angels, we meet fairies, we meet God . . .
A: Ah. Can you tell me about God? Who's he?
C: Don't you know who God is?
A: No. I want you to tell me.

C: He's the person who made the world, but there wasn't a beginning or an end of the world, but he made the world.
A: Can you see him?
C: Well, I can see him at this very moment and he's so high up. He's in a place where there's not even any air, not even colour, not even anything . . . past everything, past where there's not even colour or air. There's just nothing.
A: He's a man, is he, God?
C: He's a spirit.
A: He's a spirit.
C: He's a good spirit.
A: And is this good spirit not a man, then, nor a woman?
C: No.
A: A good spirit.
C: But if you die and go up to heaven, you can talk to him.
A: Really?
C: Yes. And go down as a spirit, as a good spirit, and get the things that are too dangerous for human beings to get.
A: How does he have time to talk to us all, if we can all talk to him?
C: Well, it's very simple. He just says the same thing to all of us. He's saying it all the time.
A: What is he saying?
C: Just one person does it at a time. It starts from the first person in the world, with their life . . .
A: That's very old. What about very old people? When they get to heaven, are they still old people?
C: They're young people. They start their life again and go down as different things. Like if I went up and I wanted to be a bird next time I came down, I would be a bird next time I came down.
A: And what would you like to be next time?
C: Well, I would like to be a bird.
A: What sort of bird?
C: I would like to be a swan.
A: A swan! Why?
C: Because they're very beautiful animals.
A: They truly are.

Do you think God may want to shape this child's beliefs as she reads the Bible? Or is her mix of fantasy and reality normal and healthy for her age? Or could both be true?

Between the ages of, say, three and eight, fantasy and reality exist together in children, neither being more nor less real, influential, important or loved. Their inner world consists largely of beliefs which their imagination has constructed, of stories they have heard and of their own, firsthand experiences of the world. Only later will they be bothered about knowing what's 'true' and what isn't.

Somewhere between the ages of six and twelve, they may begin to realise that some of their beliefs cannot coexist — they are incompatible. Alternatively, children may find it no problem to hold contradictory beliefs. Contemporary thinking doesn't demand a consistent world-view. In the eleven to fourteen age range, many decide that the Bible is no more than a story to grow out of, that some of it defies belief because it describes things which simply couldn't happen, and that it doesn't describe what real life is like. Postmodern thinking rejects any one story's ability to contain the true picture of everything that goes on in the universe.

Yet the Bible — the one story — does give the true picture of everything. Christian educator, Lawrence O Richards, calls the Bible 'God's invitation to experience reality'. If our children explore the Bible regularly, it will begin to shape their thinking and show them the reality of God at work in and beyond the life they see around them. And the sooner they start to see it the better.

As a teenager, I was fortunate enough to have Percy as a friend, and to be taught faithfully by him for four years. He knew the Bible inside out and back to front, because he had read it for sixty years and was still thrilled by what he discovered in it. His Bible was covered with green, blue and red pen marks as he linked thoughts and themes across the breadth of it.

As I talked to him towards the end of his life, I had the distinct impression that his mind and the Lord's were very close, though he himself would have said that he still had much to learn. He seemed more in touch with reality than ever. It filled me with joy to see how the obvious next step for him was to go to be with the Lord, to make the unity complete, to experience the ultimate reality, to know the truth about everything. I desperately wanted to reach that point too — my passion for God's word had been kindled, and I wanted my thoughts to be shaped by it in line with God's thoughts.

The Bible directs their emotions

More than anything else, a sense of worthlessness drains the life out of children of the 1990s. It prevents them from living courageously, from believing that they can make any lasting mark on the world, from going out and doing something instead of staying in and being passive. With little or no sense of self-worth, they can only be 'heroes' by living vicariously – as the hero of the computer game, as the rebel in the comic or on the music scene, as the saviour of the world in the video.

So much can undermine children's self-respect: feeling guilty without knowing how to be forgiven; being unheard or 'invisible' and therefore feeling powerless; being embarrassed; being put in a position where their incompetence is made public; being teased; being lonely; being treated patronisingly; not being trusted to become more independent; feeling the odd one out; being pushed to live up to impossibly high expectations; being afraid with no one to stand beside them; being abused; not being the 'favourite' . . . The list is endless. Children can begin to believe they have nothing to contribute anywhere.

Social commentator, Richard Eckersley, speaks of 'a failure to provide youth with a sense of being part of a community and . . . a deep sense of relatedness and connectedness to the world and to the universe.' Australian pastor, John Smith, observes, 'We have neglected to give children a coherent world-view, a commitment to life beyond individualism and a context of family faithfulness and tribal security. We have offered no challenge to self-indulgence.'

The Bible can help children to face this emotional hurt and overcome this deprivation: it tells them, 'God knows. He cares. You're loved. You're valuable.' The knowledge of their worth is one of the roots from which a healthy emotional life can develop. Through the Bible, God can help children not only to express their emotions, but also to direct and control them, and change their negative feelings to positive ones.

In *God-Talk With Young Children*, John Hull tells the story of two children from the same family reacting emotionally to the story of Jephthah in the Old Testament (Judges 11:30–40):

> Jephthah promised God that if he was victorious in battle, he would sacrifice to God the first living creature that greeted him when he came home. To his dismay, he was greeted by his daughter. Nevertheless, he kept his promise to God. After the parent had read the story to his daughter, the following conversation took place:

Child (about five years old): What would you have done?
Parent: What do you mean, what would I have done?
C: If you had made that promise?
P: I wouldn't have been so silly as to make such a silly promise in the first place.
C: But if you had? What would you do then, if you had made the promise?
P: If I had made such a silly promise, I would be even sillier to keep it, wouldn't I?
C: Yes. (Pause.)
Goodnight, Daddy.
(Calls out after parent has left room.)
I love you, Daddy.

The father has become Jephthah and the child has become Jephthah's daughter. The question has become one of safety and of trust, and of the place which the child holds in the affections and commitments of the parent . . . The defence of the child's sense of safety requires an attack on the fanaticism of Jephthah . . .

In the case of older young people, the question becomes one of identity and of autonomy. What bargains and contracts have been entered into behind my back? What have my parents committed me to of which I know nothing? Who am I that other people, even God, can decide my fate? In the following example, a fifteen-year-old girl had been studying Jephthah as part of her religious education at school. She burst into the living room where her mother was watching the television.

Daughter: You know, Mummy, I'm studying Jephthah in the Old Testament.
Mother: Really, dear? What do you think of him?
D (passionately): He was a bastard!
M: Oh. Why was that?
D: He didn't care what happened to her. He only thought of himself. He had to keep his promise whatever happened. It didn't matter to him.
M: Oh. I see. Well . . .

D (kneeling beside mother and bursting into tears): And you know, Mummy, we don't even know her name!

With ten years between them, both girls reacted to the story emotionally, but differently. It gave the younger one the opportunity to voice her sense of insecurity and to regain the knowledge of her self-worth; it helped the older one to 'protest against the helplessness and anonymity of the young caught in the military and political manoeuvres of the older generation', according to John Hull. Both grew emotionally through the encounter. Both became more sure of themselves.

James and Claire are two other children who have gained self-assurance from the Bible discoveries they have made. James says, 'My favourite part of 2 Corinthians is 5:1–10. I liked the bit about my life at the moment being like an old tent compared with the eternal house in heaven that God has saved for me. I can't wait to get to heaven. As a result, I feel more confident.'

Claire is full of joy: 'My favourite bit of 2 Corinthians is 4:13–18. I like it because it helps me look forward to heaven and realise how lucky I am to have Jesus as my Saviour. When I read it, I feel like dancing!'

Stephanie has been reading her Bible for about three years, and loves it. Clearly its images have stuck in her mind – she describes a dream that we would very happily call 'biblical': 'One night when I was at my boarding school, I was crying because I was homesick. I thought no one was with me and no one cared about me. I forgot all about God and cried myself to sleep. And I had a beautiful dream which I shall never forget. I was walking through a lovely jungle with one of my friends. Soon we saw a hill, a big hill, and a voice called to us saying, "Stephanie and Helen, come up here!" So we climbed the hill and we saw Jesus. He told us to sit down. Then he broke some bread and gave us some wine, and took us by the hand down some valleys where beautiful flowers were growing. There he said, "Be like this long line of flowers following the path where they have been planted." Then he blessed us, and suddenly there was a long staircase ahead of us. Jesus went up it, saying, "Remember this. I'll always be with you." Then he disappeared and we praised God for what he'd shown us.' The Bible clearly provided Stephanie with the raw material from which her dream was made.

Through the Bible, God wants children to understand their immense worth, and to experience and express emotions in positive, constructive ways rather than negative, destructive ones.

The Bible inspires their actions

Children are targeted as consumers from their earliest years. They are encouraged to become armchair superheroes, to buy, take home, enjoy and live through someone else's story. But God's word is the enemy of inactivity, apathy and self-centredness. It is action-packed – characters in the Bible don't sit at home doing nothing much! Its message is clear – life is best when we get out, get active and do what God wants. Loving God involves both inner love and trust, and outward godly action. When Bible characters are pleasing him, they are not apathetic, inactive and self-centred.

However, the Bible doesn't give children stereotyped role-models to follow. The 'goodies' don't always win and the 'baddies' don't always lose – not in this life anyway. Nor does the Bible always make clear who are the 'goodies' and who the 'baddies'. Was King David a goody? Yes, because he trusted God and tried to live to please him. But then there was the Bathsheba incident and the grisly murder of Uriah. Can we call a murderer a goody? What about Rahab? Her 'open house' for the men of Jericho was the perfect hideout for Moses' two spies – no one would suspect two strange men going there because it happened all the time (she was a prostitute). So it looks like she was a baddy whom God used for good. But then we discover her in Jesus' family tree!

Goodies or baddies – it's not easy to tell. Instead of putting characters into these unhelpful, simplistic categories, God wants Bible readers to know that even his people are imperfect and make mistakes; yet he can still use them and wants them to be active for him. He wants us to see that the more we live the way he wants us to, the better life is for everyone. So we must be very careful how we handle Bible stories with children. The 'obvious' Bible stories to use may have hidden dangers if we are tempted to make goodies completely good and baddies completely bad. Real life isn't like that. However, if we use stories as they stand without heavy editing, we help children to come to terms with real life and to play a godly part in it.

After reading her Bible, Rosie was inspired to act on behalf of someone who couldn't stand up for herself — a thoroughly biblical thing to do: 'There was this girl who moved down here from London and when she was younger she had a hole in the heart. Something that the hospital did made her very overweight and people called her "podge" and stuff. She'd go out of school crying because of what the boys had done and some of the girls as well. I got together with another Christian girl. When the boys were being horrible, we wouldn't join in. We just sort of looked at them as if they were behaving really childishly. They must have thought, "We don't want to be looked down on, so let's not do it any more." And they realised it was also hurting the girl.'

GETTING INTO THE BIBLE

We don't want children to look at the Bible superficially and bounce off it uninterested or unchanged. We want them to get involved in it physically, mentally and emotionally so that God can change them. With young children, this shaping of thoughts, directing of emotions and inspiring of actions will happen if we use the Bible faithfully and wholeheartedly, and encourage them to be totally caught up in it. Why? Because God will make sure his word achieves what he wants it to achieve. If older children are to grow in faith, they must learn to come to the Bible and even to confront God with their honest feelings, thoughts and actions. In the end, however, they have to make the deliberate effort to tell him, 'This is what *I* think — now show me what *you* think, Lord, and I'll change my mind if I'm wrong', 'This is what makes *me* angry/happy/sad — now show me what makes *you* angry/happy/sad, and I'll try to be like you', 'This is what *I* want to do — show me what *you* want me to do, and I'll put your way first. I want to love you with all my heart, soul, mind and strength.'

✎ **Reflection 1** ✎

Now here's a surprise. As soon as you can, go and find a tree by a stream. Yes, I know you only ever go looking for trees if you are taking the dog for a walk and, even then, not if it is raining. Throw your routine into total chaos and get looking. Book another time in your diary if you have to. Make sure you take a pen with you – and this book of course, or you won't know what to do next!

● Settle down beside the tree. Make yourself comfortable in a quiet place where you won't be interrupted. Start by looking carefully at the tree, to appreciate its beauty and strength. Don't worry – people will think you're bird-watching!

● Tell God honestly how you feel about reading the Bible regularly for yourself. Do you get that sinking feeling even thinking about it, because you know you should read it, but either you don't or you don't get that much out of it when you do? Or do you find it a thoroughly refreshing part of your Christian life?

● Ask God to make the following few minutes a really good experience of his word as he speaks to you through it. Then your journey won't just have been good exercise for your legs!

● Read Psalm 1 slowly, simply enjoying the central 'tree' image and your own present surroundings:

Happy are those
   who reject the advice of evil people,
   who do not follow the example of sinners
   or join those who have no use for God.
Instead, they find joy in obeying the Law of the Lord,
   and they study it day and night.
They are like trees that grow beside a stream,
   that bear fruit at the right time,
   and whose leaves do not dry up.
They succeed in everything they do.

But evil people are not like this at all;
   they are like straw that the wind blows away.

Sinners will be condemned by God
  and kept apart from God's own people.
The righteous are guided and protected by the Lord,
  but the evil are on the way to their doom.

● Underline all the phrases or sentences that tell you something about those who take notice of God's word (the 'Law').

● Use your imagination and scribble down ways in which people who love the Bible and live by it are like trees. Metaphors in the Bible stick in our minds and stimulate our imaginations.

● Pause for a few moments and think of the children who mean most to you – in your family, among your friends, in the children's group you work with. Tell the Lord how you long for them to be nourished by his word. Write their names around the psalm. Link their names with some of the tree qualities you have jotted down already.

● Read the psalm again, out loud if you can. When your eye catches a child's name in the margin, stop and pray for him or her along the lines of what you have just been reading. Then carry on reading the psalm from where you left off.

● When you have finished, make sure you have prayed for every child whose name you have written. Then pray for yourself, as you try to encourage them with the Bible.

∽ Reflection 2 ∾

First, let's allow our minds to wander a little. Imagination is a gift from God which Jesus used all the time. He saw a miserable blind man, but imagined someone who would dance for joy because he could see again. He saw the five loaves and two fish, and imagined what a party there would be if everyone could have a feast from them. And wouldn't it tell the people so much about their Father in heaven if there were stacks left over? Jesus' imagination started the miracle of change.

To say defeatedly that the children we care for will never

grow to love the Bible is inconsistent with a gospel in which every good thing is possible. Faith means keeping in mind and hoping for what we cannot yet see. A vivid imagination is fundamental to a faith that sees God do miracles. So our first small step towards helping children to explore the Bible, and to take notice of what God says through it, may be to imagine what it might actually be like if they *did*.

Tim is five now. In twenty years' time he'll be worldly-wise. We may still be able to glimpse in his features the child he was; his smile won't have changed, and his eyes will still light up when he talks about how much God loves him. But by then he'll know the pressures on him to be independent, rugged, fun-loving, 'one of the lads' — a highly-targeted consumer. Perhaps he'll be a whiz-kid in advertising, love fast cars and have luxurious holidays somewhere hot and action-packed. Nothing wrong with that! Or he may be unemployed, living in a dismal bed-sit. But he will have been meeting God through the Bible for twenty-two years, on and off.

His big sister started reading him Bible stories when he was three, and he was awestruck by a God who could do such amazing things. He always found the Bible easier when he was together with someone — in the church group or at home — and even now he struggles to read it on his own, though he does try. But he would feel 'thirsty' if he didn't hear the Bible in some way. Through it he knows God and himself. In it he sees success and failure for what they are both really worth. He's solid, in spite of what it seems like sometimes.

The stream has flowed constantly. But this is twenty years from now. He's only five. He's getting his first bike for Christmas.

Jodie is in the park most of the time. She's usually on the swing, going gently backwards and forwards, backwards and forwards, with a blank expression on her face. She had the same look when she wandered aimlessly into the holiday club that time when they were doing the story of Zacchaeus, but she never went back again. Jodie always was a loner, and now that she's twelve, her preference to be on her own marks her out clearly from the rest. 'She's weird!' some of the children at school reckon. Well, that's just their opinion.

In twenty years' time, where will she be? Who will she be with, if anyone? What will she be doing? Maybe she'll be married to someone who's never around — and be much happier like that, even if it means a struggle to bring up the children single-handedly. But she might remember the Bible story of the loner no one liked.

Maybe she'll wander into church again just for the peace and quiet. She'll discover some Bibles at the back and sit for almost an hour trying to find that story again among all the flimsy pages. But she won't be able to. So perhaps she'll slip the Bible into her bag and leave. Occasionally she'll get it out to read — when she's in bed and her husband is still wallowing in the bath. When he sees what she's reading, he'll probably tell her she's mad, but she knows she's not. Within the book's pages she'll be discovering life and the joy of being together with God, though she won't call it that. She'll hang in there with the Bible, like tree roots reaching out to the stream.

Now she's only twelve, and never goes on the roundabout because there are other people there.

Trying to imagine our own children's future will help us to pray. How might the children you care for be like 'trees by a stream' in twenty years' time? Spend some time hoping about their love of God's word and what it might mean for them. Turn your thoughts into prayer.

Alone with your vision? You don't have to be.

• With a friend or a group leader with whom you work, start by talking about your tree by the stream and how it helped you. Be frank about your concern for your children, and see what the reaction of the other person is. You will probably find he or she thinks exactly the same as you! If so, try to find a time to pray together specifically about the aim of this book.

• On the occasions when the leaders of the children's groups in your church meet together, use a different chapter of this book each time to help you evaluate your Bible work with your groups. Ask the other leaders *not* to do some of the 'Plans for growth' activities at the end of the chapter before-hand, because it may be more beneficial to do one or more of these together when you meet.

• Read one chapter a week, and do the 'Plans for growth'

activities during the days in between. Perhaps keep a diary of your discoveries. As you talk and explore with your child or children, note down any changes in attitude they have towards the Bible and any special insights they give you.

● If you cannot spend as much time on this as the three ways above would suggest, well, you have got the vision now. Wait for one of the children to say something like one of the chapter headings, and you're away! Dip into that chapter, do the activities, and pray like crazy that they will grow like sturdy trees by a stream!

∽ Plans for Growth ∾

Plan 1
With the children who will be your fellow Bible explorers, watch, listen to and read the same things they do – TV, video, music, magazines, books, comics, computer games, board games, story tapes and anything else that conveys a message.

Ask your children what they enjoy about these things, though they may not be able to put it into words. Ask yourself whether the values the different media are conveying are godly, whether they are helpful as a basis for learning about God, and whether the powerful ideas and images in them are 'true, noble, right, pure, lovely and honourable' (Philippians 4:8).

Plan 2
Over the next few weeks, go to as many groups or services as possible which have children at them, to see how the leader does the 'Bible bit' and how the children respond to it in each case. You could go to family services, pram services, parent-and-toddler groups, a holiday Bible club, midweek club night, children's Bible study home groups, a Sunday group – whatever is happening in your church during the time you allow for observing.

In each case, ask the group leader if it would be all right for you to watch because you are collecting positive ways of using the Bible. For each group, note down any child's response to what he or she hears from the Bible. Does it make anyone want to ask questions or stretch their minds about God? This is belief being shaped. Does anyone respond emotionally to it, for instance by clearly being amazed or saddened or made happy? This is emotion being directed. Does anyone get involved in activity as a result of their discoveries, either in a related game or drama, or through craft work, or even by hinting that they might want to live differently because of it? This is action being inspired.

At the end of your observation period, try to interpret your notes in terms of what you yourself could do when using the Bible with your own children or with your group.

Plan 3

Read any well-written story to a child or group of children in a dramatic way. Use facial expressions, different voices for different characters and bodily gestures to make the story come alive. As you read, try to notice how the children are being drawn into it.

Pause at the end to let the children respond in any way they like. (They may just sit there waiting for you to tell them what to do next, but they may not!) Are those who respond thinking about what happened and what it might mean? Or are they emotionally involved in it – sad, happy, frightened? Or do they burst into action copying some of the characters? Or all three? If there is silence, try asking them the following:

What did you think would happen when . . .?
Why do you think X did Y?
How did you feel when . . .?
Who would you like to have been in the story?
Has anything like this ever happened to you? What did you do?

Bible Activity 2 'Faith Shaper' (page 142) shows how to use part of the Bible with children along these lines.

∞ Chapter Two ∞

THE BIBLE AND US

NEVER SATISFIED!

This summer was horribly hot. The earth was parched, the grass a deathly yellow, even brown in places – 'drought conditions', the experts said. An apple that I had taken for lunch baked while it was in the car. The gorgeous smell of baked apple made me long for custard – cold custard.

Right in the middle of the moors, miles away from civilisation but halfway round a very popular tourist walk, we came across an ice-cream van. It must have stood there all summer, irresistibly beckoning to every passing walker – and undoubtedly making the ice-cream man a millionaire without him budging an inch!

Everyone wore shorts this summer. Apparently there was either a national shortage or cities were packing them off to the coast, so you couldn't get a pair in the West Midlands! And we all moaned about the weather.

Then, two weeks ago it started raining, and has carried on pretty well non-stop ever since! The grass has already revived, plants and trees have visibly freshened up, the leak in the gutter has registered on our consciousness again, the ice-cream man has no doubt gone home – and everyone is wrapped in winter woollies and moaning about the weather!

We are usually dissatisfied with our present experience or situation. Sometimes that is no bad thing. I believe there is a dissatisfaction built into us which comes from God himself. It makes us thirst for him, long for more of him, want to experience him in a 'more real way', knowing that nothing and no one will ever satisfy us apart from him, (Psalm 63:1). If we let our thirst drive us back to our Bibles and to prayer, later – when we explore the Bible with our children – we shall have something important to tell them about the deep satisfaction of God. We will never convince them that the

Bible is refreshing, vital and full of adventure if *we* don't find it so, if we have never longed for God with a godly dissatisfaction and found him with the help of the Bible's pages.

Taking the time to work through the answers to the following three questions may be a good way to trigger our longing for God and our excitement about exploring the Bible ourselves and with our children:

What exactly is in the Bible?
What do *we* believe about the Bible, and what are the implications of our beliefs for our Bible exploration with children?
How can we best explore the Bible for ourselves?

WHAT EXACTLY IS IN THE BIBLE?

The Bible is the vast story of God the King's relationship with his people; he shows them who he is and how they can stay close to him, and this sends a message to the rest of the world about what he is like.

Though the Bible contains the true life-stories of many people, and was produced by more than forty different authors over a period of more than 2,000 years, it also tells the one panoramic story of how God creates, judges, shapes and saves his people. And, though the Bible is one epic story, there are two testaments or 'covenants' within it – the Old Testament and the New Testament.

The Old Testament begins at Creation, when God the King simply said the word and everything burst into existence, including human beings. (Even before Creation, God had planned to make people his own through Christ.) God loved the people he had made and wanted them to be close to him; but they decided to rebel and go their own way.

Many years later, when the people of Israel were slaves in Egypt, God rescued them, showing that he was a much greater King than the king of Egypt and all his weird gods! As they travelled through the wilderness towards the land he had promised them, God the King made a covenant ('testament' or 'agreement') with his people, and gave them rules for the best kind of life – the Ten Commandments and other laws. As he ruled the nation of Israel, he wanted his people to obey him and show the rest of the world what he was like. He was their God, and they would be part of his plan for them and for the whole of creation. But the Israelites often messed up; they disobeyed God and endured much suffering in wars and in exile. Yet God the King never gave up on them. Amazing! His covenant was always that of one-sided love.

Then came the greatest promise imaginable. God said that one day his Son would come into the world and reign for ever. In the New Testament, we discover how God fulfilled his promise of salvation through Jesus, his Son, who showed everyone exactly what God was like. Jesus proclaimed the arrival of the kingdom of God and died so that everyone could be part of that kingdom. By the Holy Spirit, God spread his kingdom throughout the world, and he is still doing so. God will finally establish his kingdom and gather all his people together to be with him in heaven for ever. The Bible's story isn't over yet.

God has chosen to tell us this story through many different kinds of writing – stories and histories, law, wisdom, poetry and song, prophecy, Gospel episodes, letters or epistles, and visionary writing. (Many Bible books have more than one kind of writing in them.) You will have the opportunity to sample these for yourself in the 'Plans for growth' in chapter seven. Between them, these different kinds of writing sharpen our minds, touch us emotionally and prompt us into the best way to live, drawing us all the time towards God. Each kind of writing should be explored in the particular way that will help us to get at the story behind the words and to see God in it.

Bible Activity 3 'Place Setter' and Bible Activity 4 'Way Finder' (page 145) suggest ways to help children find their way around the Bible.

WHAT DO WE BELIEVE ABOUT THE BIBLE?

Some of our beliefs about the Bible are outlined below. Listed under each are some of the implications that this belief has for our exploration of the Bible with children. Add more of your own as you think and pray through your beliefs.

Both the Old and New Testaments reveal God and his love for us, as one whole story

• We will be careful to look at both the Old and New Testaments with our children.

• We will expect to meet God in some way on every page and to be amazed by his love.

• Jesus is at the heart of the Bible. Essentially, the Bible is about who Jesus is, what he has done, what he is doing and what he will do. We will often talk about Jesus with our children when we explore the Bible together.

....
....
....
....

The Bible is totally reliable

• When faced with something we don't understand in the Bible, we will tell our children that we don't know rather than cast doubt on what the Bible says.

• We must work hard at what the Bible means ourselves so that we don't teach as 'totally reliable' something that turns out not to be true and which our children have to unlearn later.

....
....
....
....

The Bible was given by the Holy Spirit

• When we explore the Bible with our children, it should be a significant spiritual event.

• If the Holy Spirit gave the Bible to us, we should ask him to help us understand it before we explore it.

....
....
....
....

The Bible is the true word of God

• We will expect God himself to speak to us and tell us what he wants us to know as we explore the Bible.

• When God speaks, we can expect our own and our children's lives to be changed. We cannot come face to face with God and stay the same!

• The Bible contains many different styles of writing, so our children will need help to recognise the difference between these and to handle each in the right way.

• The Bible is God's word expressed through human authors and cultures, so we must try to understand both their world and ours if we are to hear faithfully what God is saying.

....
....
....
....

The Bible is intended to lead us to salvation

• Since the Bible is about being forgiven through Christ, we will focus on the good news more than on the bad, though children should know God as the one who both loves and judges.

• We will often talk with our children about our own Christian lives: for example, what Jesus did for us through his life, death and resurrection; what it means to be forgiven.

....
....
....
....

The Bible shows us what Christian faith and lifestyle look like

• We will tell our children that we too are people who are growing in faith. We make mistakes and don't have all the answers. We are learning.

• We need to make sure that our children can see us living out daily the Christian life we discover in the Bible.

....
....
....
....

The Bible tells us authoritatively what the church should be like

• We will try to relate what we discover to what we see happening among God's people in the local, national and worldwide church. Our children need to know that there are many Christians around who are trying to do what the Bible says.

....
....
....
....

∽ Reflection ∾

You may want to use the following outline of Scripture Union's *Aims, beliefs and basic philosophy* to help you pray through some of your thinking.

Working with the churches, Scripture Union aims . . . to encourage people of all ages to meet God daily through the Bible and prayer . . .

We believe that the Old and New Testament Scriptures are God-breathed, since their writers spoke from God as they were moved by the Holy Spirit; hence are fully trustworthy in all that they affirm; and are our highest authority for faith and life.

One of the other emphases which binds the Movement together is on the importance of the Bible in the life of a Christian, and on teaching him to read it regularly, thoughtfully and systematically. Such reading is not seen as an end in itself but as leading to repentance, faith, worship and obedience, and to a balanced understanding of its teaching.

A prayer for children's Bible exploration

Lord, we pray that our children will rush to hear and respond to your word, not because they are forced to but because they want to.

Please help them to be sure that, whichever part of the Bible we are exploring together, the words hold what you, Lord, want our children to know. These words won't turn out to be lies but truth by which they can safely live their whole lives.

So, Lord, help us to handle your word with our children in such a way that they will long to be drawn into it often and be so engrossed in and shaped by thoughts that are your thoughts, that they never grow out of your word but are always growing into it. May they be like 'trees by a stream' that display your glory throughout their lives.

Now get together with someone else who has tackled this exercise, and compare notes. If there are beliefs and implications about which you disagree, ask your church leader for help.

HOW CAN WE BEST EXPLORE THE BIBLE FOR OURSELVES?

We must develop a thirst for God's word

We must come to the Bible vulnerably, as people in desperate need of hearing from God, because this is exactly what we are. We must come to the Bible openly, flood defences down, ready to be refreshed, made alive, changed by what we hear God saying through it. This is vulnerability that recognises the authority of God's word.

Why should exploring the Bible change us? Because it reveals God to us. It shows us who he is, what he is like, what he has done, is going and will do, what he wants and what he doesn't want – and we can't truly meet with him without being changed by the experience.

ᴄᴐ **Reflection** ᴄᴐ

Go and fetch a glass of clean, fresh water to drink. Sip it
slowly as you read these words from the Bible. As you do,
imagine the rain and the snow – perhaps especially the snow,
so rare in Israel. Try to picture the scene in your mind:

> 'My word is like the snow and the rain
>> that come down from the sky to water the earth.
> They make the crops grow
>> and provide seed for sowing and food to eat.
> So also will be the word that I speak –
>> it will not fail to do what I plan for it;
>> it will do everything I send it to do.
>
> 'You will leave Babylon with joy;
>> you will be led out of the city in peace.
> The mountains and the hills will burst into singing,
>> and the trees will shout for joy.
> Cypress trees will grow where now there are briars;
>> myrtle trees will come up in place of thorns.
> This will be a sign that will last for ever,
>> a reminder of what I, the Lord, have done.'
>>
>> (*Isaiah 55:10–13.*)

When God says these words to his people, they are in exile
in Babylon, becoming settled, losing the cutting edge of
their vision, and no longer responding to the fact that they
are God's covenant people. God is reminding them that his
word – in this case his call to them to repent – isn't an added
luxury item; it is like vital irrigation for dry lands.

We must discover the way in which we prefer to learn from God's word

Think about yourself. How do you best relate to what you
discover in the Bible, and how do you learn from it? Is it
through the study – working out the implications as you
grasp the theological issues and try to understand everything
you read? Or by being silent and listening to God, meditating
on the text, allowing yourself to be moved by what you
read? Or by latching onto how the different characters lived
and trying to live like them (or not like them!)?

There are suggestions to help with each of these three
approaches in 'Resources' (page 188). Write to the various

publishers for their current catalogues of Bible reading guides, to see which suits you best. Your local Christian bookshop may also be able to advise you on what is available.

When you want a change, why not try an approach to the Bible that you don't normally use? For example, if you are someone who prefers a 'study' approach, try meditating on some verses or taking a Bible character as a role-model instead. We all have our preferences, but we do need to have balance, to challenge us and keep us from falling into a rut. Think about how you could change your Bible reading method occasionally.

Reflective, creative approach

Use a Bible guide like *Alive to God* (Scripture Union).

Try biblical meditation, in conjunction with a study approach. Meditation really means mulling Bible verses over and over again (as in Psalm 119:97).

Combine music, pictures and verses of Scripture (eg a psalm). Focus on the words and images that are used, whilst playing peaceful music on tape.

Have a go at memorising short passages of the Bible, so that you can continue to 'chew them over' any time, anywhere.

Practical, hands-on approach

Try *Daily Bread* (Scripture Union).

Use a paraphrase (like *The Message* by Eugene H Peterson, published by NavPress) beside your usual Bible version, to help you experience the immediate impact of the verses.

Look in your local Christian bookshop for recordings of unabridged Bible text. Listen to a whole Bible book in the car or around the house, to 'get under the skin' of what God is saying through it.

Study approach

Ask your church leaders for details of home groups that focus on Bible study.

Become a member of a tape library. You could try: All Soul's Tape Library, 2 All Soul's Place, London W1N 3DB; the audio library at St Helen's, Bishopsgate, St Helen's Vestry, Great Helen's Street, London EC3A 6AT; or Anchor

Recordings, 72 The Street, Kennington, Ashford, Kent TN24 9HS. Others are listed in the *UK Christian Handbook*.

Use commentaries. Especially readable are 'The Bible Speaks Today' series. Find out from your friends which commentaries they have, so that you don't have to spend a lot of money.

Use Bible study notes like *Encounter With God* (Scripture Union).

If you are not used to thinking of the Bible as the one big story of salvation, some books may take your breath away, eg *According to Plan* by Graeme Goldsworthy (Lancer/InterVarsity Press, 1991) or *Get Into the Bible* by John Richardson (MPA Books, 1994).

We must build a structure for spending time with God around his word

This is important for developing the habit of regular Bible reading. The structure you follow will depend to some extent on your preferred approach to the Bible. Many Bible reading guides suggest ways of using their material.

Here is one example of how you might structure your time with God:

PRAY

. . . that God will speak to you as you read his word, and that the Holy Spirit will help you to understand and respond to what you read.

READ

. . . the Bible passage carefully, listening for what God is saying to you.

THINK

Explore the meaning of the passage with the help of these questions:

What is the main point of the passage?

What does it teach us about God — the Father, his Son Jesus Christ, and the Holy Spirit?

Is there a promise or a command, a warning or an example to take special notice of?

How does this passage help us to understand ourselves, our situation or our relationships?

PRAY
With your discoveries in mind, use the reading to help you worship God and to pray for yourself and others.

SHARE
Decide how to share what you have learnt with other people — in words and in practical action.

> Bible Activity 5 'In Touch' (page 147) is a way of using the basic structure outlined above with children.

Planning your structure will mean that you put aside a reasonable time each day, or each week. Think about your lifestyle. When are you at your brightest? Is there a 'window' in your daily or weekly schedule when you can sit down to read without interruptions? It need not be at the same hour — nor even be the same amount of time — each day or week, if that isn't practical for you.

Don't feel constrained about the kind of structure or the time of day you choose. There are all sorts of ways of getting into God's word. Listening to a tape on your Walkman on the train to work may be the right one for you.

∽ Chapter Three ∾

'IT'S GOT NOTHING TO DO WITH REAL LIFE'

ROOT PROBLEM

'Why don't people of your age bother with the Bible?' I asked a group of eleven- and twelve-year-olds. They thought carefully. First, they gave the more straightforward answers which showed that life was too full and too pressurised to bother:

'It's long and boring.'
'I don't have time.'
'Everyone makes it sound so serious.'
'The writing is tiny.'

Then the more thought-provoking replies:

'It's not relevant. It all happened such a long time ago.'
'So much of it doesn't seem to matter.'
'*I've* never experienced anything that happened in the Bible.'
'I don't need it.'
'We're not Christians.'

The Bible simply doesn't seem attractive or relevant to them. It is a 'voice' which, one way or another, they are sure they don't need to hear.

The group's early comments were about how hard it is to read the Bible. Their later observations focus on how easy it is to reject the Bible as having nothing to do with real life: there is not enough in it that is identifiably related to them; it's about people who are different. The Bible spans different centuries, countries and climates. It's full of wacky names, values, social and religious customs. The group can't make head nor tail of what's happening on the political scene in the historical bits. It seems as if you would have to be a masochistic mental contortionist to make any sense of it at all, let alone see yourself reflected in it. Not attractive, not relevant, just not them.

I am privileged to have met Mark. Aged ten, he had the kind of face that spelt mischief. People just couldn't help liking him. His eyes shone as he blurted out his latest joke. He would pop up at unexpected moments, asking if he could help.

He was so alive — at times, at least. He was living with his father who wasn't a Christian but who was as proud of Mark as any father could be. Perhaps the knowledge of this fact gave Mark his short-lived bursts of confidence.

At other times he was the loner. His face clouded over as if he were remembering all he didn't have. He walked down the lane by himself or sat in the corner with his feet up on a chair doing nothing.

I don't really know how Mark came to be on the holiday activity we were leading. He didn't come with friends; he wasn't part of a Christian group; he didn't go to church very often. He was just there. He would sometimes struggle to get into the Bible by himself (he wasn't brilliant at reading), but even if he managed to handle the words, he didn't really understand what they meant nor what kind of life they were describing, nor when or where it was all supposed to have happened. Worse, he said that whichever bit of the Bible he stumbled into, he got the feeling that it was 'always telling him off'; so he never really enjoyed it. Eventually he gave up — there was more to be lost than gained by attempting to read it.

The difficulty for us wasn't in getting Mark to explore the Bible for the first time, but to dare to explore it again.

After the holiday he wrote to us: 'If we don't read our Bibles, can we still go to heaven? I hope so because I'm still useless at reading mine, but I do want to go to heaven.'

Oh no! Was this really the message we had given him?

How can we get our children to read the Bible and to discover that it's about real life and isn't just a way of earning a place in heaven? Should we drag them shouting and screaming to the Bible? Or should we wait until they show the first glimmer of interest and dive in with them enthusiastically at that point? Every group leader or parent who is keen on their children exploring the Bible has asked this question at some time or other. Not being sure of the answer and often in desperation, we try a variety of tactics.

Coercion ('You *will* read it') is the approach some take, but it rarely has a lasting effect. As soon as the threat is removed, Bible reading stops. Coercion encourages action without involvement.

Guilt isn't much better ('Read your Bible or you'll make God sad', 'Read your Bible – it cost me an arm and leg last Christmas'). If it works at all, it makes enjoyment of Bible discovery almost impossible. If children don't read it, they are displeasing someone; if they do, they are displeasing themselves because the reason for doing it is to get it done!

We can always try fear ('It's a sin not to read your Bible'). A group leader in North Hornsey, London, wrote in the newsletter *Children's Scripture Union: Hints and Encouragements, 1889:*

> I am sure that the daily Bible reading is a great blessing to many of the dear children, and in nearly every case it is conscientiously carried out. I heard of one little girl, after her light was put out at night, crying bitterly because she had forgotten her reading, and begging for a light for fear she should be turned out of the union.

Clearly, in 1889, instilling this kind of fear in children was acceptable, and telling this particular story was seen as an encouragement to others. The important thing was to bring children into contact with the Bible by whatever means possible!

However, there was some good news around in 1889 too. A group leader from Plymouth wrote:

> I used to have a Bible Class, alternately with a Sewing Meeting when I read a story to the children instead. But finding they wished for the Bible Class always, the Sewing Meeting was discontinued.

The moral of the story is that, if we want to get children exploring the Bible, we should offer sewing as an alternative! But here we see a glimmer of the motivation in children that can result from caring, adult encouragement.

Let's go back twelve years further still, to witness the start of what was to become the Children's Scripture Union:

In 1877 a girl of eighteen or twenty, Annie Marston . . . went to live with the family of Canon Harford-Battersby, who a few years earlier had founded the Keswick Convention. She took a class of small girls in the Sunday School, and encouraged them to read the Bible on their own during the week, with little success. 'I have tried, over and over again,' one child would say, 'but I could never keep on! . . . There were such long lists of names, I couldn't even read them, so I gave up' . . . 'I got to such difficult chapters, I couldn't understand them, so I gave up.' Miss Marston wrote out weekly for each child 'a list of portions to be read daily until the following Sunday, on the understanding that during morning school we would talk about the difficult parts, and they might ask questions freely. Very soon they became so eager, and their questions were so many and sometimes so important, though their ages were mainly from eight to ten, that it was impossible to get through in the limited time at our disposal.' (From *The Good Seed* by J C Pollock.)

It was a wonder that Mark ever found his way into the Bible at all, and no wonder that he struggles with it. One key factor was missing that might have helped him to be excited about the Bible, to handle it, to understand it and to relate it to his own life – an adult's undivided attention. Mark had no comfort, security or encouragement from someone who could help him be brave enough to keep on making observations or asking the right questions, or simply to relax and enjoy a good story. At the point where he felt particularly vulnerable – faced with a huge, unfamiliar book – he had no one to prevent him failing with it. The fact that it didn't seem to be about real life didn't make the risk worth taking.

'Snuggle-up' value

Some of us have lingering, vivid memories of snuggling up with a parent and a story book at bedtime – precious, unhurried moments of undivided attention, long-awaited, long-cherished. No doubt the stories stayed with us longer and the images remained fresher in our minds because of the warm, loving atmosphere in which they were explored. The story book had 'snuggle-up value'.

The Bible can have 'snuggle-up value' too (but not a physical 'snuggle-up', unless it is parents with their own children). The Bible is a brilliant book to read with someone we love and trust. Trying to understand it together is what God intended when he gave the Bible to the community of his people. Close, warm relationships are vital when we are exploring strange, sometimes threatening territory, when we want to ask some of life's biggest questions, when we want to laugh or cry, or when we simply want to sit and wonder, but not alone.

However, there is much more benefit in adults and children exploring the Bible together than just this 'snuggle-up value', as important as this is.

GROWING TREES

Those special moments – when ordinary, daily life and the words on the page match up and spark off each other – seem to happen more often for children when there is someone beside them to prompt and help them. This relationship may be that of a child and his or her parents or adult friends, or that of group members and a caring group leader. These special moments seem to happen less often when children explore the Bible on their own, though of course they should be encouraged to learn to listen to God for themselves.

Right priorities
Without an adult's help, Mark wouldn't see that Bible exploration was a top priority for someone who wanted to get to know God better and live his way.

Right perceptions
Without an adult's help, Mark's perceptions of the Bible couldn't be shaped. If all his experiences of it were bad news, he couldn't be expected to discover that its message was actually good news.

Right skills
Without an adult's help, Mark couldn't gain the right skills for exploring the Bible. *We* know that there are brilliant, exciting stories in the Bible, and one huge story behind all the others,

but Mark never could know – the stories were closed to him. *We* know there is amazing variety in the Bible – poetry, prophecy, history, fascinating details of law – but it all looked the same to Mark. There was a whole world to discover there, but he couldn't find the way into the adventure.

Much of this book is about equipping children with the skills they need to explore the Bible in a group or by themselves. At this point we simply need to note that we must *beware* of using the Bible with children in a way that makes them totally dependent on the presence of an adult or a group. We must encourage them to do alone what we do with them. Of course, there will be some who struggle with books and reading and literacy skills; but it is always possible for us to give them something that they can take away and do on their own, something, for instance, that they can memorise and meditate on at another time and in another place. It will help to keep in mind that our times together with children and the Bible are essentially times of training.

> Bible Activity 6 'Not Just Words' (page 149) suggests ways of presenting the Bible to children who are not so happy with reading.

However, helping children to love the Bible, to overcome the difficulties they have in understanding it, and to be thrilled and moved by what they read or hear, is more than just a matter of explaining to them how important the Bible is or what it is really like, or finding clever, entertaining ways to tell a story or explore some Bible verses. Undivided attention and the encouraging of right priorities, perceptions and skills will never be enough.

In the time that an adult and child spend together, the most important factor is that the message of the Bible is being lived out by the person the child is with.

God at work right here

Mark had probably never seen anyone moved, challenged or excited by the Bible. As far as he was aware, no one had ever said, 'Hey! That's amazing!' or 'That's terrifying!' or had wanted to respond to the Bible by talking to the Person described in the verses. How else, apart from seeing the clear impact of the Bible on adults, will children know that everything it contains is about real life and, even more amazing, about *their* real life? No amount of talking and training will communicate that the Bible is totally relevant if our own lives don't match up with what God says through the Bible.

The Bible makes most impact when it is explored with someone in whose life the truth is clear. To be honest, if *we* are not thrilled by what God has given us and is saying to us in the Bible, if our lives do not reflect the reality found there, we may as well give up trying to help our children with it. Either they will see through us and refuse to have anything to do with the Bible, or else they will read it and begin to understand that the Bible is something we pretend about – it is boring really, but we say it is exciting! Our children's attitude to the Bible is caught, not taught.

Our role

Percy was my Bible-loving leader when I was fourteen. (I've mentioned him before.) There were just four of us in the group, seated every week on the same hard chairs round the same bare kitchen table. Patiently, Percy taught us to handle the Bible with skill, making sure that individually we could grasp the aspects of Bible discovery that we found hard.

For one term, he retold us the story of the book of Acts from his open, annotated, used-to-death King James Version of the Bible. Yes, he retold the story very dramatically before we found it in our Bibles. That way he could tell the story of his own life in parallel on the way through. There was no run-around quiz, computerised scoreboard or gunk tank; but we were riveted, drawn into the story by the fact that Percy clearly believed every word of it, staked his whole future on it and was simply full of it. What he was telling us was matched by his life. His enthusiasm, and then ours, arose from the realisation that the Bible was the place where he was brought face to face with God. We couldn't deny the reality of what was happening before our eyes. The Bible story and the God the Bible is about was living there for us – in him.

When asked how they saw their roles when exploring the Bible with children, a group of adults drew up this list: friend, leader, guide, director, listener, encourager, teacher, arbiter, adviser, counsellor, provider of energy and security, rewarder and Bible interpreter. Yes, we probably need to be all these and more when we read the Bible with children. But don't worry – if we are living God's word ourselves, we shall probably be most of them without really trying!

∾ Plans for Growth ∾

Plan 1

Try not to rush the time you spend with your children looking at the Bible. For frantic parents or group leaders with a million and one other things to achieve, this may seem a bit idealistic. But if you do find yourself rushing, is there another part of your programme or your day that you can shorten or lose completely? Ideally, after your reading or presentation of the Bible story or verses, a time with the Bible should last as long as our children's enthusiasm for it lasts.

Plan 2

One by one, focus on each of the words listed by the group leaders above to describe our own role with children when we explore the Bible together: friend, leader, guide, director, listener, encourager, teacher, arbiter, adviser, counsellor, provider of energy and security, rewarder and Bible interpreter.

In your mind's eye, picture yourself in each role during a Bible session with the children you are thinking about. How have you been that role, or how would you like to be it? Think very practically.

Where do you sit, stand or kneel?
What kind of expression do you have on your face?
What tone of voice do you use?
How do you respond when a child gets something wrong?
What is there about the role that you struggle with?
What do you get enthusiastic about?

What makes you cross?
What really encourages you?

Turn your thoughts into prayer.

๛ **Chapter Four** ๛

'I'M BORED WITH IT'

ROOT PROBLEM

'Boring!' We hear the word used all the time when reality doesn't match wish, dream or fantasy, when anticipation outshines actual experience. Children always seem to need Action Factor Five Million. 'Boring' means 'nothing special is happening'.

But of course children never call the Bible 'boring', do they? They are *always* wildly enthusiastic about reading or hearing it. We have just got into the bath when there's a knock at the door — they want us to do more Bible with them! We are in the car, and all they want to listen to is the Bible story tapes — forget all that chart rubbish! We are getting the room ready for our Sunday group, and already the children are bursting in clutching their Bibles and asking excitedly, 'Which bit is it this week?' We are in church, and they are sitting on the edge of their pews just waiting for the Bible reading and talk . . .

Some dream! The reality is — well — rather different!

'Do I *have* to read it?'
'I read it last month!'
'OK, but only for two minutes!'

We wince as we hear ourselves saying things like 'I'll give you money if you read it!' or 'It'll help you pass your exams!' or 'If you don't do it, I'll belt you one!'

Usually children will stick with the Bible while they explore it with adults in whose lives the Bible message is real and obvious, and who make it (or the activity that goes with it) fun, exciting, entertaining, challenging or useful. As some young Bible readers said:

'The best bit of the Bible is the Psalms, because I like poems. They cheer me up.'

'I like Judges because it describes the vicious circle that people can get themselves into.'

'The crossing of the Red Sea is amazing!'

'Mark's Gospel is great because I've read it all!'

'I like the story of Ruth best because I can understand it better than the others.'

'The story of Samson knocking the building down is really exciting!'

'I enjoy Proverbs best because they're really good advice.'

'1 Corinthians 13 is good because it's all about love, and people need to learn a lot about loving and caring.'

Not bad as far as it goes, but there has to be more to Bible exploration than fun, excitement, entertainment, challenge or usefulness. Even these wear thin pretty quickly.

According to a 1993 survey *Reaching and Keeping Teenagers* by Peter Brierley (Marc), the biggest single cause of young people leaving the church in the United Kingdom is that 'worship services are boring'. In other words, the experience is supposed to be something brilliant, but turns out *not* to be. The presence of God was promised but, judging by the lack of action, he didn't show up. Nothing special happened. 'Boring!'

One reason why children sometimes find the Bible dull may be that we adults often build it up to be a pretty amazing book (which it is!), perhaps even the 'Speaking-God book', but for our children it turns out to be a million pages of tiny, black print – the world's biggest, hardest comprehension exercise. Again, God doesn't show up. Nothing special is happening. 'Boring!'

Where is God?

The Bible is God's unique revelation of himself through history, designed to bring us face to face with him, and it contains the response of ordinary human beings to this revelation. Children need to know this sense of the Bible's 'specialness', so that they get past the black print on a page and meet God there. Let's go for 'fun', 'excitement', 'challenge' and 'usefulness' (all good things to enjoy about the Bible), but let's also hope for children to be filled with 'a sense of awe'.

'I like Revelation because it encourages me to think that God's plan is still working.'
'The words of Psalm 23 tell me that God is always with me.'
'I like John 3:16 because, even though some people don't care about God, he still cares about them.'
'When I've read John 14:1–14, I realise again that God really loves me and that there'll be a place for me in heaven.'
'My favourite part of the Bible is when Jesus rose from the dead, because it shows what a great King he is!'
'I'm always reading about Noah's ark because the story shows someone's faith in God and how powerful God is.'
'Ephesians 3:16–21 is my favourite part because God gave me these verses when I was healed of asthma.'
'I like Luke 12:22–31 best because it helps me feel I can trust God for everything.'

Do you sense the awe in these comments and the awareness that the Bible is about our *real* God at work in our *real* world and our *real* lives, that the almighty Lord of all history is interested in and involved with individuals, loves them and cares for them? Staggeringly, God's vast salvation plan, carried out over thousands of years, includes children of the 1990s and twenty-first century. That is awesome!

However we explore the Bible with our children, we must not simply rely on our relationship with them nor on the entertainment value of any Bible activities we do with them. We must simply expect and allow for the sense of awe that they will experience when faced with God himself at work. American writer, Linette Martin, warns us:

> A child comes to us with a capacity for glory and wonder, for amazement and awe, and for tremendous, wordless joy. What do we do with their priceless gift? We systematically brutalise it with pocket-sized ideas.
>
> 'Jesus,' we tell him, 'is just like your elder brother.' The child is puzzled. Only that morning his elder brother kicked over his pile of Lego bricks, and the child slugged him, and they

both got yelled at and told to go and get ready for Sunday School and church.

'God is like your daddy,' we tell the child. Again, he is puzzled. He loves his daddy and chats to him about many things. But isn't God somehow . . . *bigger* than that? The child's head tilts and his brow wrinkles. 'Oh, no,' we insist, smiling down from an adult height, 'God is Abba-Father, just like your daddy. You can talk to him just the same way.'

We have been carefully taught not to confuse Little Minds with ideas that are beyond their reach. Make things easy for Small Minds. Explain all the mysteries of the faith in terms of everyday life. Play guitars and tin whistles. Make sure the kids have lots of fun.

Yes, it all sounds most reasonable (and so it is), but it is tragically and horribly wrong. In our proper concern to teach Christian doctrine, we are cheating our children of the one thing that doctrine is about: the reality of God.

One of the great men of the church spent years writing theology, then he had a vision of God's glory. He said that all his writings seemed in comparison like straw. Well, straw is what we are giving our children . . . Some of them never grow up to where they were before. (From 'Children Fed on Straw', *Third Way.*)

One reason why children *don't* keep going with the Bible is that they stop (or never even start) being awed by the God they discover through its pages. Jesus made it clear that he didn't want people to be narrow-minded, with little sense of the greatness of God.

The blind and the crippled came to him in the Temple, and he healed them. The chief priests and the teachers of the Law became angry when they saw the wonderful things he was doing and the children shouting in the Temple, 'Praise to David's Son!' So they asked Jesus, 'Do you hear what they are saying?'

'Indeed I do,' answered Jesus. 'Haven't you ever read this scripture? "You have trained children and babies to offer perfect praise." ' (*Matthew 21:14-16.*)

In effect, Jesus was saying, 'I want everyone – pilgrims, the blind, the lame, children – to be able to meet with God and worship him here. And you – exploiters and religious hierarchy – I want you to help, not hinder them.'

Through the Bible, children can meet with their awesome

God. He has addressed the Bible – his revelation of who he is, what he is like, what he has done, what he is doing and will do, what he wants and doesn't want – to our children as well as to us. We want them to know the Bible as something bigger than they are, because it tells them more than they knew, speaks of things more mysterious than they could imagine, shows them themselves in a light in which they have never seen themselves before. And, above all, the Bible introduces them to a God who is much more powerful and loving than they ever thought.

GROWING TREES

So how can we explore the Bible with children in a way that will help them to come face to face with God and therefore avoid the boredom factor? Key aspects are:

● A sense of anticipation that we are looking at a special book in which we *expect* to come face to face with God. We must pray for this to happen.

● Looking for God on every page, asking and answering the right questions about him and being filled with awe when we meet him.

● Full involvement in discovering the truth as we encourage children to use explorers' skills with the Bible, as we identify with their struggles, affirm their contributions, and guide them towards a good understanding.

● Helping them learn to see their own life stories as part of the vast epic of God's word, as we show children the reality of God at work in our lives.

● Allowing our children to respond to the God of the Bible in worship, which might include prayer for help, confession, thanksgiving, shock, praise, puzzlement, sadness, adoration, silence, laughter – an almost endless list! A child should not be forced to respond to the Bible in a particular way. In fact, we must not try to force *any* response to what they have discovered, though we can help children to see what kinds of response are possible:

When Bible exploration time is over, we should clarify with the children what we have discovered together. Our big questions about God (page 63) will help with this.

Ask the children what all this makes them want to say to God, if anything. Give them the opportunity to say it: allow for responses of prayer, praise, confession, awed silence, joyful laughter, tears, quiet thoughtfulness . . . Join in yourself with a response based clearly on the Bible verses.

Ask the children what difference their discovery might make to their lives. We cannot *dictate* the difference it might make, but we can suggest aspects of their lives that might be affected: for example, their lives at school or at home, the way they treat their friends or do their homework, what happens when they go to their school Christian group. Many will not know, and this is fine. Others *will* know, and they will get excited about the difference and want to keep on talking about it. Don't crush their enthusiasm with your adult 'realism'.

Give specific examples of how, through these verses, God has changed the life of someone you know, including yourself! This gives the children a model of how the biblical text can be applied to real life.

Do not expect every Bible exploration to end in the children's values and lifestyle being turned upside-down. God does demand change through the Bible, and we must not underestimate a child's ability to live a thrillingly radical Christian life; but change and growth are normally slow.

None of this could be called 'boring'! At least, I haven't yet come across anyone who has met God and thought the experience a bit of a yawn! When children sense this 'specialness' about the Bible and are brought face to face with God through it, we can know for certain that the Holy Spirit is at work, because he 'reveals the truth about God' (John 14:17). He takes who the children are and the way they operate, and works it together with what they hear or read in the Bible so that the reality of God impacts on them.

However, his role is much more than the phrase 'bringing the Bible alive to children' suggests. The Holy Spirit wants to do everything necessary to 'lead them into all truth' (John 16:13).

The Holy Spirit's role

Perhaps you would like to change pace a little, and use this section as a time of prayer for the child or children you have been focusing on as you read this book. What we want children to do and be may all sound hopelessly idealistic. Well, it is 'idealistic' certainly, but never 'hopeless'. We will be praying to the God who can make impossibilities happen (Mark 10:27).

A Bible verse will help us to focus our thoughts, and then to pray that the Holy Spirit will do for the children each of the things mentioned above.

> In my desire for your commands
> I pant with open mouth.
> (Psalm 119:131.)

The Holy Spirit is the one who will give children a sense of anticipation, taking away any sense of pending boredom when they open the Bible's pages or settle down to hear it being read. Under his influence they will wait to be enthralled by seeing in action the God who loves them deeply.

Pause for prayer.

> 'Father, Lord of heaven and earth! I thank you because you have shown to the unlearned what you have hidden from the wise and learned. Yes, Father, this is how you wanted it to happen.' (Matthew 11:25–26.)

The Holy Spirit works with children's 'unlearnedness' to show them God. Even with all the intellectual difficulties that the Bible presents to them, we should expect the message often to be more obvious to children than to adults, and for them to see God in places where we have missed him.

Pause for prayer.

> The word of God is alive and active, sharper than any double-edged sword. It cuts all the way through, to where soul and

spirit meet, to where joints and marrow come together. It
judges the desires and thoughts of the heart. (*Hebrews 4:12.*)

The Holy Spirit breathes life into the Bible verses, so that
the children are drawn deeper into them. Children respond
to the same God they meet in its pages; they are thrilled to
live with him and ready to be changed by him.

Pause for prayer.

'The Helper, the Holy Spirit, whom the Father will send in
my name, will teach you everything and make you remember
all that I have told you.' (*John 14:25.*)

'When, however, the Spirit comes, who reveals the truth about
God, he will lead you into all the truth. He will not speak on
his own authority, but he will speak of what he hears, and will
tell you of things to come. He will give me glory, because he
will take what I say and tell it to you.' (*John 16:13–14.*)

The Holy Spirit makes the connections between the Bible
verses and the children's lives, turning 'words' into 'the word
of God'. He jogs memories, links images and blows the dust
off things already known about God which have been stored
away in their consciousness. He points children to Jesus and
helps them to think about their lives with him.

Pause for prayer.

Those who are led by God's Spirit are God's children. For the
Spirit that God has given you does not make you slaves and
cause you to be afraid; instead, the Spirit makes you God's
children, and by the Spirit's power we cry out to God, 'Father!
my Father!' God's Spirit joins himself to our spirits to declare
that we are God's children. (*Romans 8:14–16.*)

Children may not respond to the Bible in the 'tidy' way that
adults do. However, all the time the Holy Spirit will be
building the special relationship between our Christian
children and God.

Pause for prayer.

On the last and most important day of the festival Jesus stood
up and said in a loud voice, 'Whoever is thirsty should come
to me, and whoever believes in me should drink. As the
scripture says, "Streams of life-giving water will pour out from

his side." ' Jesus said this about the Spirit, which those who believed in him were going to receive. (*John 7:37–39.*)

The Holy Spirit helps the word to 'live' and to 'remain' in children, so that this word makes the world of difference to the way they live.

Pause for prayer.

> [The disciples said to each other,] 'Wasn't it like a fire burning in us when he talked to us on the road and explained the Scriptures to us?' (*Luke 24:32.*)

If our children are to keep going with the Bible, we must pray that they too will experience the 'burning' realisation of the reality of God, which the Holy Spirit brings.

Our role

So, how can we be more helpful to the Holy Spirit in all this? Let's focus on the first two vital aspects of Bible exploration with children that I have listed on page 59 – a sense of anticipation, and looking for God on every page:

• We can pray with children before we ever open the Bible, asking God to tell us something special about himself and about our own lives.

Bible Activity 7 'This is It!' (page 152) suggests ways to pray with children.

• We can help children to look for God in the Bible, and to be awestruck by him, asking the following kinds of questions and providing them with gentle hints in the comments we make:

Who does this part of the Bible tell us God is, directly in the words or because of the kinds of things he is doing or saying?

What is God like in this passage?

What has he done? Or what is he doing now? Or what *will* he do?

What does God want?

What doesn't he want?
What might it be like to live with this God?

Now we won't, of course, go through this checklist of questions each time we read the Bible with our children, but in every part of it we should get into the habit of looking with them for our real God at work in our real world and in our real lives. In chapter five, we will see how we can help them to use their explorers' skills to discover for themselves the answers to these questions.

> Bible Activity 8 'Magazine Cut-up' (page 154) gives an example of how the questions listed above might work; and Bible Activity 9 'Life Books' (page 156) offers a way of helping children to see that the Bible is *everything* to do with real life.

∽ Plans for growth ∾

Plan 1
Write on a piece of paper the questions listed above that help us look for God in the Bible. Read the verses you will be using with the children next time you get together, or read the verses assigned to that day's session in your Bible reading guide. Then make a note of your own responses to those questions. Get into the habit of looking for God yourself in the Bible.

Plan 2
If your children call the Bible 'boring', draw a line under the vital aspects of Bible exploration that you think might be missing for them:

A sense of anticipation (this chapter, so get working at it!).
Looking for God on every page (this chapter again!).
Their full involvement in discovering the truth (chapters five, six and seven).
Learning to see their own life story as part of the vast epic of God's word (chapters eight and nine).
Response to the God they discover there (chapter eleven).

Go straight to the appropriate chapter of this book as noted in the brackets. Then look at the practical activities in chapter ten that will help you with the particular problem you have pinpointed.

Chapter Five

'I CAN'T UNDERSTAND IT'

ROOT PROBLEM

Wise Owl flew down to the ground from the hole in High Tree which had been his cosy home for many more years than he could remember. What a superior bird he felt today – like most days! 'Whooo, whooo!' he hooted with delight, ruffling his feathers to give himself the stature he felt his status deserved. As it was now getting dusk, the rest of the wood needed to be aware that he had arrived back on the scene and was in control once again.

He had seen all the life there was to see in the wood, and had no reason to believe there was anything beyond. My word, he'd experienced some goings-on in his time and each of them, he believed, had added immensely to his already considerable wisdom.

As he drew a circle on the ground with the tip of his wing, other woodland creatures came out to see what he was doing. Wise Owl encircled both the tree and himself with the line in the dirt, and began writing, in large letters, 'S-O-M-E-W-H-E-R-E S-I-G-N-I-F-I-C-A-N-T'. Then, outside the circle, he painstakingly completed the words 'N-O-W-H-E-R-E W-O-R-T-H M-E-N-T-I-O-N-I-N-G'.

When he had finished, he settled himself down on a lower branch of High Tree and looked pleased with himself, especially since, with relatively little effort, he had managed to attract the attention of so many other animals and birds.

When he felt that a large enough audience was gathered outside his circle, he cleared his throat with a 'Whu, whu, whooo' and began. 'My dear friends, I know all there is to know and I want you all to know it too,' he hooted. 'There's no reliable knowledge that doesn't come through me. Only the Owl flies high enough, sees far enough and lives long enough to know about life here in the wood, and this seems much too good an opportunity for you to miss.'

'But . . .' squeaked Molly Mouse.

'Just wait a min . . .' began Ferdinand Fox.

'Firmly fixed to the ground as most of you are,' continued Wise Owl, without hearing any interruptions, 'you cannot even see what I have written in the dirt here. No, you have to be up high!'

The other animals and birds fell into a hushed reverence. They had an equally good view of life in the woods from the ground up, but they were quickly discovering that this didn't count . . .

A group of ten- to thirteen-year-olds were asked individually which parts of the Bible they found most helpful. Almost all of them said they got most out of those parts which told them categorically that God loved them (for example, 1 John), that Jesus was on their side (the Gospels) and that they should behave in a specific way (Proverbs or some sections of the epistles) – in other words, parts which communicated simply and directly. The words on the page were easy to understand and their meaning was clear. Seeing it from the other perspective, one of the twelve-year-olds said that some people don't read the Bible because it 'doesn't always mean what it appears to say'.

Many parts of the Bible are, of course, hard to understand or, if not to understand, to interpret. I wondered, however, if well-meaning adults had deterred this twelve-year-old from even attempting to get to grips herself with the harder parts of the Bible because they had always presented as the 'right answer' an interpretation that they themselves had arrived at after years of study. Might not the girl's own understanding and interpretation have been equally valid if only someone had encouraged her and listened carefully to her?

Children will sometimes have clear insights into the Bible which we adults have missed, and we must learn to value these highly. Then our children will have the confidence to build even greater insights onto those they already have. The best response to the child's claim 'I can't understand it!' may be 'Well, have a try. Go on, tell me!'

Here are some unaided interpretations of the Parable of the Mustard Seed. The children, largely from a church background, understood the story because it was easy, and were then asked to say what they thought it meant. Watch how the interpretations change from age to age.

> Jesus told them another parable: 'The Kingdom of heaven is like this. A man takes a mustard seed and sows it in his field. It is the smallest of all seeds, but when it grows up, it is the biggest of all plants. It becomes a tree, so that birds come and make their nests in its branches.' (*Matthew 13:31–32.*)

They were all asked precisely the same question: 'What is the story about?'

Four-year-olds
'Jesus.'
'A seed.'

Eight-year-olds
'Birds making their nests.'
'It's like life. When you plant a seed in Jesus and you become really good.'

Twelve-year-olds
'Something that starts small and gets big.'
'When you give a little something and it becomes a whole lot more.'
'It's like when we start off loving God and learn to love him more and more.'
'Everyone in the world having the chance to become Christians.'

Sixteen-year-olds
'The mustard seed is God's word and it can be planted in the heart of any person, however influential or not. And from that it grows as the family of God grows and reaches out, and the birds represent more people who come and feed off the word, and multiply the Kingdom of God.'
'The word can take a small thing like the mustard plant, like a weak person, and can change him or her into something strong like a tree. So even a weak person can reach out – something they wouldn't dream of doing unless they had God's word inside them.'

The next question was 'Why did Jesus tell the people this story?'

Four-year-olds
'Because he wanted to tell them about a seed.'

Eight-year-olds

'To show them his love.'
'To ask them if they wanted to become Christians, but not forcing them.'

Sixteen-year-olds
'To show that each of them had the ability inside them to spread the word, and that they needed God – they couldn't do it on their own.'

We should be able to stand back from most of these interpretations and say, 'Yes, the four-year-olds have got something right and helpful to say, and so have the eights, and so have I.' If we put all the interpretations together, weeding out those which are clearly not right and cannot be backed up from other parts of Scripture, we have a richness of meaning far beyond what any one person at any age could offer. Children *can* understand the Bible, and their interpretation of it should be valued along with our own. We must resist the temptation to ruffle our feathers and act as if they have remained in 'Nowhere Worth Mentioning'.

GROWING TREES
Children have always been involved in the revelation of the truth about God to the world, and in the serious, 'adult' business of helping people respond to his love. God has always wanted to reveal the truth about himself to children:

> [God said,] 'Remember these commands and cherish them. Tie them on your arms and wear them on your foreheads as a reminder. Teach them to your children. Talk about them when you are at home and when you are away, when you are resting and when you are working. Write them on the doorposts of your houses and on your gates. Then you and your children will live a long time in the land that the Lord your God promised

to give to your ancestors. You will live there as long as there is a sky above the earth.' (*Deuteronomy 11:18–20.*)

[John said,] 'I am writing to you, my children, because you know the Father. I am writing to you, fathers, because you know him who has existed from the beginning. I am writing to you, young people, because you are strong; the word of God lives in you, and you have defeated the Evil One.' (*1 John 2:14.*)

God has also wanted to reveal the truth about himself *through* children:

O Lord, our Lord,
  your greatness is seen in all the world!
Your praise reaches up to the heavens;
  it is sung by children and babies.
      (*Psalm 8:1–2.*)

As we saw in Matthew 21:14–16, the children in the Temple saw exactly who Jesus was and shouted it out loud, while some of the adults around them hadn't got that far in their understanding. People may consider children to be 'unlearned' and 'foolish' (Matthew 11:25), but Jesus said that they were valuable and had just the right qualities for understanding the 'secrets' of God:

Jesus called a child, made him stand in front of [the disciples], and said, 'I assure you that unless you change and become like children, you will never enter the Kingdom of heaven. The greatest in the Kingdom of heaven is the one who humbles himself and becomes like this child. And whoever welcomes in my name one such child as this, welcomes me.' (*Matthew 18:2–4.*)

When they read or hear the Bible, children bring to it many helpful attitudes and skills, just because of the way they are. Later on as adults, they may have to re-learn some of these attitudes and skills as tools of good Bible interpretation. For instance, they have:

A sense of expectation and awe

Children explore unknown Bible 'territory' expecting that anything at all can happen. They are on an adventure with God, and he can do any mind-boggling thing he likes. And when he does, children gasp, if not audibly then inwardly.

We should continue to encourage this sense of awe in our children, and they should be able to teach it to us.

Humility

Children don't normally come to the Bible with many pre-conceptions – as adults might – or with any attempt to justify their lifestyle, or find ammunition for their own argument, or hear 'a word from the Lord especially for today'. They trust the Bible to say what it means. Younger children often unconsciously accept its authority as they eagerly wait to see what it will tell them this time: they take the words at face value. Older children may not be so accepting.

Their capacity for enthusiastic exploration and this infant vulnerability mean that the Bible will often have far greater impact on children than we adults allow it to have on us. Thankfully, twelve- and thirteen-year-olds can just about hang on to, or relearn, this kind of humility towards the Bible, as the following prayers show:

'Lord, I like the Bible because it's you telling me how to live on earth properly and how to get to heaven.'

'Thank you, Lord, because without the Bible my life would be a confused mess.'

We adults need to relearn this humility towards the text, not in the sense of simply understanding everything naïvely at face value (God's word always means more), but in the sense of being willing to be astounded and changed by what we read.

Honesty

Imagine. Uncles, aunts and long-lost cousins have all squashed into the front room for the family Christmas party. Suddenly, in a quieter moment, a five-year-old pipes up: 'Is it as boring as you thought it would be, Mummy?' There's a stony silence . . .

We have all cringed at children's honesty, spontaneity and lack of inhibition when they have asked searching but embarrassing questions, or have come out with the perceptive but not quite polite comment. Why couldn't they just keep quiet? Well, it's because they are children and they want to be sure about things.

This honesty is exactly what we all need when we explore the Bible – the honesty that will allow us to make any comments at all about it, or any heart-felt response. Children have not yet learned that there are certain comments we don't make about the Bible and certain responses we don't have – praise God! When we admit and voice our honest comments or responses, whatever they are, we will have got rid of pretence. We will be opening ourselves up to God and his word with an appropriate boldness, expecting our real God to shape our real lives.

Curiosity

'Why didn't God help them?'
'I thought God loved everyone. So why did he have those people killed?'
'What's circumcision?'
'Why do you make it sound so boring, Daddy?'
'How did the baby Jesus get inside Mary's tummy, then?'
'Why do we have to read this bit?'

Out of sheer curiosity, children often ask the obvious, face-value questions about the Bible.

Sadly, we adults have largely stopped asking questions about the Bible. Instead we want to 'master it', and use it to increase our knowledge and to help us give answers. Perhaps we are secretly afraid that the Bible won't stand up to too much honest interrogation, so we need to protect it by curbing our curiosity. Maybe we feel it is somehow not polite to ask God tough questions about what's in it. But there were many characters in the Bible who asked God honest, in-your-face questions that may sound impertinent to us:

Moses: 'When I go to the Israelites and say to them, "The God of your ancestors sent me to you," they will ask me, "What is his name?" So what can I tell them?' (Exodus 3:13).

Gideon (to an angel of the Lord): 'If I may ask, sir, why has all this happened to us if the Lord is with us?' (Judges 6:13).

Job: 'Speak first, O God, and I will answer. Or let me speak, and you answer me. What are my sins? What wrongs have I done? What crimes am I charged with? Why do you avoid me? Why do you treat me like an enemy?' (Job 13:22–24).

Mary (to the angel Gabriel): 'I am a virgin. How, then, can this be?' (Luke 1:34).

These questions actually proved to be turning-points in the lives of these characters, in their faith and the way they served God.

Acquisitiveness

I can't believe that, even with all the hi-tech entertainment imaginable breathing down their necks, plane-spotters still exist; but they do – I've seen them! There they all were at Birmingham airport last Sunday afternoon scribbling down aircraft registrations, flight numbers, destinations, arrivals, delay times, reasons for delay – you name it, the information was somewhere in those dog-eared notebooks.

Children also love to collect things and can be pretty single-minded about it – posters of their latest hero, signatures, matchboxes from around the world, weird trivia about things that no one in the world is interested in, car hubcaps . . . But this acquisitiveness is exactly what anyone needs to interpret the Bible well. Children find it much easier than adults to take in details of a part of the Bible and what it says about God, and to store the information until it is needed. As we discovered earlier, one of the keys to good interpretation is to let the Bible interpret the Bible – in other words, to match what we believe it says in one place with what we know it says somewhere else. This is the way to build up a knowledge of God and of ourselves. In this kind of activity, children have a head start.

'Holes in the ground' was the trigger-idea when I started to read the Old Testament story of Joseph to our four-year-old:

Lucy: Someone put Daniel down a hole too, didn't they?
Me: Yes, with lions.
(Pause.)
Lucy: But God got him out of there.
Me: That's right, he did.
Lucy: God gets Joseph out of this one too, I remember.

Perhaps a study of biblical holes in the ground would lead us to much greater depth in our understanding of God's care!

Imagination

Only recently have some Christians woken up to the fact that imagination may be a good thing in helping us to explore the Bible. Earlier, the use of the imagination and the skills of meditation were sometimes considered dangerous and therefore to be avoided; the 'opening of the mind' could lead to the Devil taking possession and making people think his thoughts (or their own) rather than God's. Yet meditation should be a characteristic of the spiritual mind:

> I remember the days gone by;
>   I think about all that you have done,
>   I bring to mind all your deeds.
> I lift up my hands to you in prayer
>   like dry ground my soul is thirsty for you.
>   (*Psalm 143:5–6.*)

Whilst there is a danger of misinterpretation with unguided meditation, we now feel much more at ease with 'entering into' Bible stories and using Scripture to focus our thinking. Of course, children are brilliant at imaginative play, at pretending to be the hero, at recreating a whole series of events in drama; and this is exactly what God invites them and us to do in order to live what is in the Bible. It is as if he is saying, 'I'm the main character here, but put yourself in the position of this character and that character. What did I do in their lives? So what do you think I might want to do in yours?'

If we adults could find the right way to enjoy this 'imaginative play' with the Bible, along with our usual ways of studying it, we might be able to make the vital connections more easily and read ourselves into the biblical text much more than we do.

When it all goes wrong

When children (and adults) explore the Bible, they automatically match what they read or hear with what they already know about life, the world, the church, God, themselves, their families and friends. Subconsciously they ask, 'If it doesn't match, which is wrong? The Bible? Me? God? My friends?' Then comes the flood of questions.

Yet their views may be skewed from the truth, and their understanding and interpretation of the Bible based on unreliable information. For instance, when he read about Jesus dying on the cross, one boy exclaimed, 'God must have really hated Jesus to let him die like that!' You see, that is what life is usually like – people hurting those they hate. Christians can also add to the confusion when they don't think before they speak. I once heard of a leader who closed an evening session at a children's camp with the prayer, 'We thank you, Father, for dying on the cross for us . . .' No wonder children get confused!

Children will interpret the Bible, and their interpretation will be coloured by what they know and by what is happening to them; our task is to allow them or help them to interpret the Bible correctly.

Ten-year-old Tim was worried. 'It says in 1 John 3:9, "Whoever is a child of God does not continue to sin, for God's very nature is in him; and because God is his Father, he cannot continue to sin." Does this mean that, as soon as I became a Christian, I should have stopped sinning? I didn't. I carried on. This must mean I'm not a Christian, mustn't it?'

Ah, he hasn't understood. He has understood the words, but has interpreted them wrongly. Understanding and interpreting any part of the Bible will always mean comparing it with other parts of it. So when children get it wrong, we can react in at least two ways. Either we can ignore what they have said and quickly tell them the correct understanding and interpretation. Or we can applaud the correct interpretation and understanding they have reached up to this point, and ask them more about what they have said and why they have said it; then we can show them other parts of the Bible which may help them to question their own assumptions. But we must look for rightness first if we are ever to encourage our children to explore the Bible and make sense of it for themselves.

Up to this point, Tim had done a good job of understanding and interpreting the Bible. He had a clear image of God and of his offer of life through Christ. But his latest discoveries didn't seem to fit with the image he had so far received. Did this mean he had only reached 'Nowhere Worth Mentioning'? No, his question 'This must mean I'm not a Christian, mustn't it?' actually tells us how much of a good job he had done so far in understanding and interpreting the Bible. The answer he would find to his own question, with our help, would prove to be the next phase of his 'good job'. It would broaden his theology and give him even sharper tools with which to do the job in the future.

Learners together

Children, then, have natural abilities that can help them to discover the truth in the Bible, if we allow them to use their abilities before we insist on giving them answers. Not that they have nothing to learn from adults – no, God has begun to reveal to us the riches from his word which we shall be desperately excited to pass on to them. But, perhaps more often than we do, we should expect children to be *our* teachers, as their natural, God-given abilities and the work of the Holy Spirit in them bring us clear, new insights.

However, there are more attitudes and skills that we must help our children to gain if they are to understand the Bible better (for example, recognising what sort of Bible book a text comes from and so asking appropriate questions about it). We shall deal with these in later chapters. Meanwhile, if Wise Owl could only stop hooting for a while . . .

∾ **Plans for Growth** ∾

Plan 1

Note down as many things as you can remember of what your own children or the children in your group have taught you from the Bible. If there is a long list, thank God for speaking to you through the children.

If there aren't many, ask yourself why not. Because you have a short memory? Because you don't really think of your children as being able to teach you anything? Because your times with them are so frantic that you can only just survive, let alone listen to them? Because your children don't say anything? Because you haven't found a way of tapping into what they are really thinking?

Plan 2

Think back to the last time you used the Bible with children and consider the following:

How many minutes did you spend filling in the background to the Bible verses in however simple a way?

How many minutes did you all spend together listening to the Bible verses?

How many minutes did you spend explaining what you understood by the verses?

How many minutes did you spend listening to, reading or looking at what the children understood from the verses?

As you think through the content of this chapter, are there any changes you need to make in the way you normally handle the Bible with your group or family? Make a note of any aspects that need to be rethought for the next time you are with the children.

Bible Activity 10 'Scribble Around' (page 157) will help you to see just how able your children are as Bible explorers. It may also suggest an approach which you can adapt to use on different occasions when you explore the Bible with children.

~~ Chapter Six ~~

'I'M NOT INTERESTED'

ROOT PROBLEM

I just couldn't face another class of eleven-year-olds griping: 'We've done this bit!' I had not been teaching long, so I had never before met such a negative reaction to the Bible. I simply didn't expect it. A take-it-or-leave-it attitude wouldn't have surprised me, but totally closed minds were something else! Bible stories were what little kids did, and they had done it all at primary school. There wasn't much use in saying, 'Yes, but . . .' Prejudices were deeply rooted. There was no way the Bible was going to teach this lot anything!

This was the first time I threw Bible stories back at a group and said, 'Well, *you* do something with them then! *You* make them come alive!' And gradually they did, turning the classroom into a 'Philistine versus Israelite' battleground, huge sheets of white paper into a Superman-style cartoon-strip of the raising of Lazarus, and the corridor into a first-century slave market for the story of Philemon and Onesimus.

Sometimes the results of throwing the stories back at children and asking them to communicate the biblical truths have been amazing. Writing the message of a parable into another story with the same meaning can be pretty stretching:

From the day the acorn falls to the ground, it surrenders itself to nature's forces. But it is never alone. The wind, rain and sunshine care for it.

If someone picks it up or a creature eats it, the acorn's life is over. But if it continues to develop, the cycle of life and the nutrients of the earth enable it to grow. In time, as a new tree, its roots hold it securely in the ground.

Later the tree will, in turn, produce more acorns and eventually, after many years, the small acorn will have developed into a magnificent oak tree.

(Naomi, aged ten)

A man was shaping a clay pot on a wheel. On his first attempt, the clay wouldn't do what he wanted it to do, and the pot collapsed.

But the man didn't give up. He started the wheel again. This time the pot didn't collapse, but it didn't really look like a pot at all. Still the man didn't give up, but kept working patiently.

Every time he tried, the pot looked better and better. In the end, the pot was exactly as he wanted it to be. 'Ah,' he said, 'It's so good I'll take it home for myself.'

(Jill, aged twelve)

Our children's understanding of life and of the way a good story works is clear. Usually they are just waiting for the right information, stimulus and opportunity for this understanding to be released. Add to this the grasp of God's ways that children with a Christian background may have, and fresh, breathtaking insights into the Bible are not far away. Take 'The Messiah Rap', for instance!

'You've **heard** a load o' **raps**
About **things** that are **cool.**
Well, **this** one's on the **proph**ets –
Dead **cool** and no **fools!**
Go back in **time** several **centuries**
We're **talk**in' 'bout **years** that are **lab**elled 'BC'.
Strange things were **happ**'ning **all** those years **a**go
And the **OT proph**ets were the **dudes** in the **know.**
There was **Jer**emiah, **Zech**ariah, **Mic**ah and Isaiah –
All of them **proph**ets with their **hearts** on **fire.**
(There were **actu**ally many **more**, but **not** to be a **bore**,
We've **real**ly been **good** and have **only** listed **four.**)
For **those** of you who **find** it really **hard** to be**lieve,**
Listen to some **news** you just **gott**a re**ceive.**
Jesus' birth was **all** in God's **plan**
And **God** told it **through** the Old **Test**ament **clan.**
The Messiah would be **born** in **Beth**lehem.
Mary was his **moth**er but she **was** a **vir**gin.
The **peo**ple all be**trayed** him which **was** a great **loss.**
Then he was con**demned** and **sent** to the **cross.**
He was **taunt**ed and **mocked**, then **put** to **death**,
But **then** he came **back** . . .

[*Pause, then say slowly*]
. . . The Messiah from **Naz**areth.'
(By Jeremy Dolton-Smith and Bennett McGhee,
both aged thirteen)

Since those early teaching days, I have taken this way of
working to ludicrous extremes! Once there were seventy
of us on stage, singing the reprise of one of the production's
main songs. Then huge applause, congratulations all round,
speeches, lights down and finish. Phew! We had done it!
'Challenge Esther' had been a great success.

Three days earlier, there had been nothing but an idea of
the story-line of the book of Esther, some rough scripts of a
few scenes, and fifty unsuspecting eleven- to fourteen-year-
olds. Then came the news that in just fifty-four hours'
time, an invited audience was coming to watch a first-rate
production of the whole of the book of Esther. We had to
put on a show that faithfully represented what we found in
the Bible.

Already, after some thorough grounding in the history,
geography and culture of the Persian Empire, and in the
purpose of the book of Esther, the children themselves had
blocked out all the scenes of the story (without knowing
why), and had rewritten the dialogue to include their own
understanding and interpretation of what was going on.

'You've explored the Esther story and know it inside out.
Now, what part can you play in communicating it in a really
memorable way to the audience that will soon be here?' we
asked.

There was a few moments' hesitation in case this was all
a practical joke, but then the penny dropped and we were
off! Everyone opted for a job that they knew they could do.
We made sure there was something for everyone in putting
together the show, which we called *For Such a Time as
This* – script-writers, actors, set designers and builders, stage
managers, extras, a props department, costume designers and
makers, a video crew to record all the frantic preparation
and the production itself, programme writers and producers,
a prompt, line coaches, song-writers, musicians, a sound and
lighting crew, caterers, a front-of-house team, tea-boys and

squash–girls, car park attendants, a choir, a make–up team . . . you name it!

In case you're not too sure of the plot, here's how the programme synopsis turned out:

Basically, King Xerxes (Xerx for short, sounds like 'Zerks'!) summons Vashti HRH to him. She refuses to come. He gets mad. Big troubs! Memucan advises Vashti HRH 2 be replaced with another HRH. Search empire for beaut girls to be brought 2 palace (Spurs!) and have beaut treatment. Esther taken 2 palace – big troubs!! She's a Jew! Esther summoned 2 Xerx who fancies her. Haman (king's PM) says 2 Xerx, Jews R danger 2 empire. Haman proclaims all Jews 2B slaughtered. Jews not too chuffed. Esther takes life in her hands, goes 2 see Xerx. Invites him and Haman 2 banquet × 2. Haman reckons he's dead important. Mordecai (Esth's uncle) ignores him. Haman's ego nose-dives. Plans gallows 4 Mord. Esther rumbles plot. Haman hangs. Mord gets his job! Issues decree that Jews can defend themselves and kill enemies (clever lad!). Day 1 = 500 killed; Day 2 = 75,000 killed (enemies, that is). Mord's decree was event 2 remember. Still celebrated by Jews today, called Purim.

Got the idea? No! You should have seen the show! No one who was involved lost interest or felt they had grown out of this part of the Bible. They weren't bigger than the story, with nothing else to learn from it. The story was much bigger than them – pretty daunting, in fact! – with a vast, unknown world to explore, understand, interpret and represent.

GROWING TREES

When I was eight, our class teacher was very strict, with a military manner that demanded rigid discipline. He never invited us to ask questions or make comments, just to give precisely correct answers as he stood over us flexing his jaw muscles. We never really contributed anything of ourselves. Craftwork was carried out to detailed diagrams and measurements, creative writing to a series of set formulae. I don't recall receiving any encouragement from him, but I do remember how small he made us feel when we answered wrongly. We respected his authority out of fear and obligation – his desk drawer concealed a gym-shoe that stung. We learnt something certainly, but when that year ended, none of us went back to his room or spoke to him if we could help it. We stayed well away.

When I was nine, our class teacher was completely different. She asked us what we thought and helped us to express how we felt about things. She watched and listened carefully, and knew when we were upset. She encouraged me to start playing the violin – there were only four of us in the group. We did huge, colourful friezes, I remember, which involved covering our hands with paint. We spent hours learning multiplication tables together, and somehow enjoyed it. I have a warm feeling towards them even now! She too had real authority – we certainly did what she told us. But no one ever wanted to leave her class. As long as we were at the school, we would drift back to her room at playtime or lunchtime, to see if she wanted any help. We existed, we mattered.

We must help children (or anyone) to explore the Bible in such a way that they don't lose interest, but will always want to go back and back to it. God's word will then stay with them. The psalmist experienced this – 'How I love your law! I think about it all day long' (Psalm 119:97). God's word stayed with him so that he could recall it at any time of day or night and think about it. If this is to happen for our children, we must get the learning mix right.

In our desire to keep children interested, perhaps we haven't worked hard enough at being true to the Bible. Sometimes we have twisted the text to say something God never meant it to say, in the hope of making it easier for children; or we haven't expected the text to mean anything very much to them. We have undersold the Bible.

Perhaps we haven't worked hard enough either at being true to our *children*, at understanding the way they operate, and at being open to the new insights they might be able to give us. Generally, we have expected too much or too little of them. But our children won't return to a learning experience that either doesn't stretch them or else makes them fail. Are we selling them short?

American psychologist, Carol Dweck, gave children some

easy problem-solving tasks and recorded how they tackled them. Then she gave them some exceptionally difficult tasks and noted their behaviour. This revealed two distinct types of child.

The first group (in which there were more girls) had been good at the easy tasks, but had gone to pieces faced with difficulties. This group had been encouraged always to go for the 'right answers' and to be 'successful'. Soon the children in this group lost confidence and started to mess around.

The second group seemed to enjoy the difficulty of the more demanding tasks. Even though they couldn't solve the problems, they continued to perform well, trying to use the skills and information they had – and they enjoyed the process of learning. They didn't feel they had to get all the answers right, but they wanted to keep going, even in the face of difficulty.

Hopefully, we shall encourage our children to use and develop explorer's skills with the Bible, with less of an emphasis on getting quickly to the right answers and to 'success', and more on helping them be confident in the use of their skills and to enjoy the struggle and excitement of discovery.

Explorer's skills

When we lose our innocence – when we start feeling the weight of the atmosphere and learn that there's death in the pot – we take leave of our senses. Only children can hear the song of the male house mouse. Only children keep their eyes open . . . they have highly developed 'input systems', admitting all data indiscriminately. Matt Spireng has collected thousands of arrowheads and spearheads; he says that if you really want to find arrowheads, you must walk with a child – a child will pick up everything. All my adult life I have wished to see the cemented case of a caddis-fly larva. It took Sally Moore, the young daughter of friends, to find one on the pebbled bottom of a shallow stream on whose bank we sat side by side. 'What's this?' she asked. That, I wanted to say as I recognised the prize she held, is a *memento mori* for people who read too much. (From *Pilgrim at Tinker Creek* by Annie Dillard.)

Children are natural and gifted explorers. We must let them explore the Bible as exuberantly as they can, if they are to know that they have made a valuable contribution to the exercise of listening to God together.

Even back in 1889, Scripture Union group leaders were asking children to read, write, draw, colour and stick. In Hornsey Rise, North London . . .

> The children have made Scripture Clocks, Bible Sun, Moon and Stars, drawn and filled in with texts, a Gospel House covered with texts illustrating different parts of the house, and a Gospel Ship with texts filled in, bringing in the words 'Jesus', 'Lord' and 'Ship'. Prizes, in the shape of books, are given for the best done, and we trust by these means our boys will be led to study their Bibles, and to find the precious truths hidden therein.

Hurray for the dedication of those leaders and to the objectives they set! They were probably well ahead of their time in Bible-teaching techniques. Clearly their idea of a good time was getting the children to copy out verses of the Bible and stick them to attractive and exciting-looking features of the solar system and means of transport! Given the way children learn in the 1990s, I've got a sneaking suspicion we have to try a bit harder than that. But let's pause a moment to ask ourselves if our Bible activities with children boil down to any more than reading, thinking, remembering, writing and drawing, colouring and sticking! Sometimes these skills alone don't immediately help children to answer the big questions about God which we focused on in chapter four:

Who does this part of the Bible tell us God is, directly in the words or because of the kinds of things he is doing or saying?

What is God like in this passage?

What has he done? Or what is he doing now? Or what *will* he do?

What does God want?

What doesn't he want?

What might it be like to live with this God?

Have you ever tried writing a list of the abilities and characteristics most children have? I have, and failed, as you see!

Thinking
questioning
observation
curiosity
appreciation
reading
imagination
fascination with
words
reasoning
ready belief

Feeling
sense of fun
sense of
humour
rapport with
others
self-confidence
enjoyment of
stories
feelings
trust
enthusiasm
sense of fairness

Doing
movement
problem-
solving
team-work
sight
hearing
sense of smell
taste
touch
writing
sense of rhythm
and rhyme
measuring
drama/
pretending
improvisation
experimenting
painting/
drawing
craftwork
honesty
playing
imitating
balancing
high energy
level

Can you think of five more general abilities or characteristics that children have? Add them to each of these three lists.

Often, the more senses and abilities we can encourage children to use, the closer they will get to discovering the answers to these questions, and the more the content of the Bible will sink in and stay with them. Full involvement in learning is the first step towards the application of the biblical truths they are learning. If they are using their whole bodies to learn these truths, children will be closer to putting those same truths into action in their lives, beyond the learning context.

When we explore the Bible with children, we should try

to use as many of these skills or characteristics as possible, to help them answer the big God questions. First, we must assess what our children can do, perhaps using the above list as a guide. As we have noticed before, it is good to encourage them to use a mix of 'doing' skills (for simply seeing or experiencing what is there in the verses), 'thinking' skills (for understanding the text), and 'feeling' skills (for identifying with the mood or the characters, or for being moved emotionally).

But there are other key exploration skills that we will need to teach because they don't come quite so naturally to children. Chapter seven introduces the skills necessary for exploring different types of Bible literature, for example story, poems and prophecy. For now we will stick with helping the children to use those skills they probably already have.

Building windows in the house

For children, the Bible can seem like a dark, horrible house without any windows or doors, and they themselves are shut inside. But each time we help them to experience what is in the Bible by using one of their natural aptitudes (a sense of awe, humility, honesty, curiosity, acquisitiveness and imagination, see chapter five) or their explorer's skills (listed above), we help them knock a few bricks out of the wall and build a window in it.

Through this window they can see God's truth, the vast landscape outside. The more windows we build the more opportunities we give them to see exactly what the truth looks like. But we can only help them look — we can't make them *see*. Only the Holy Spirit can do this.

In Bible Activity 11 'Big Day Out' (page 159) we will look at part of the Bible and see how we can 'build windows' and encourage our children to 'look out of them' using their explorer's skills. We will try to do this in a way that keeps their interest, makes them feel valuable, shows them they haven't grown out of the Bible, and brings them face to face with God by discovering answers to the big God questions.

Now this could take a long time, so let's make it a family (or group) fun day. Yes, why not a whole day? What message about the Bible are we giving our children if we always squash reading it into five or ten minutes? Not every Bible discovery session needs to take a whole day, of course, but working with this time-scale might help us see more of the possibilities when we have to choose what to do with children in a shorter space of time.

⌁ Plans for growth ⌁

Plan 1

Observe your own children at play, or the children of some friends, with their agreement. Watch for as long as you can and join in if the children want you to. Notice:

Any skills they use.

Any activity that gives them immediate pleasure.

Any that gives them a great sense of achievement.

How long they spend on each activity before they get bored and move on to something different.

When you have time, think through the implications of your observations for the Bible exploration you do with your own children.

Plan 2

Children learn a lot about God, the world and themselves by asking searching questions and by getting good, honest answers, at an appropriate level, from adults. Asking questions and taking in answers are important explorer's skills which we need to encourage. But it is also important for us to ask children the *right* searching questions, either in discussion about part of the Bible or else (often more productively) when they are engrossed in another activity.

Asking the right questions, however, won't guarantee that they buzz with God-given insights, but it will definitely be a way of helping our children to express any insights they have. We will also be that much closer to finding out what is or isn't going on with them. Real communication can begin.

There are six types of question which may be helpful with children. Once we have learnt the purpose of each question, and worked out the right kind of wording, we will find that they come up much more easily in conversation, until we are asking the right questions automatically.

Let's focus on part of the Bible to help us sort out the different types of question.

> [13]Our brothers and sisters, we want you to know the truth about those who died, so that you will not be sad, as are those who have no hope. [14]We believe that Jesus died and rose again, and so we believe that God will take back with Jesus those who have died believing in him.
>
> [15]What we are teaching you now is the Lord's teaching: we who are alive on the day the Lord comes will not go ahead of those who have died. [16]There will be the shout of command, the archangel's voice, the sound of God's trumpet, and the Lord himself will come down from heaven. Those who have died believing in Christ will rise to life first; [17]then we who are living at that time will be gathered up along with them in the clouds to meet the Lord in the air. And so we will always be with the Lord. [18]So then, encourage one another with these words. (*1 Thessalonians 4:13–18.*)

The first three types of question will help us explore the verses, to see what is there:

• Factual questions, like 'What happened soon after Jesus died?' or 'Who will go to be with Jesus first when he returns?' Factual questions are good for helping children relax into giving answers and for bringing out basic information that other children in the group can learn from. Some of our big questions about God (page 84) are factual, for example 'What does God want?' or 'What doesn't he want?'

• Closed questions, like 'Will there ever be a time when Christians aren't with Jesus?' or 'Did Paul, the writer, want the people who heard his letter to be happy or sad?' Closed questions limit the number of possible answers. You may answer 'Yes' or 'No' to the first example above, and 'Happy' or 'Sad' to the second. Again, closed questions help children who aren't quite so confident at voicing their opinions to get something right, and therefore to gain confidence. Closed questions are also a good way of checking on what the children have learned.

• Open questions, like 'Why do you think some people were sad?' or 'What will happen when Jesus comes back?' Open questions help us to see what general impression our children have of what is in the verses, and also encourage wide-ranging discussion. Some of our big God questions are open, like 'What do these verses tell us about God?'

The next three types of question will help children to see that the Bible verses have something to do with their own lives, and will encourage them to respond to what they have discovered:

• Experiential questions, like 'Have you ever been really sad?' or 'How do you feel about Jesus coming back?' Experiential questions help children to relate what they have discovered from the verses to their own lives, and to get to know others in the group better.

• Rhetorical questions like 'Won't it be brilliant when Jesus comes back?' or 'Isn't it great to know that we'll be with Jesus for ever?' Rhetorical questions are not that useful – they tend to put words in the children's mouths. Occasionally, we can use these questions as a way of expressing our own response to what we have discovered.

• Leading questions like 'Do you think there's any good news in these verses, David?' or 'If I asked you to draw something from these verses, what would you draw, Rebecca?' Leading questions are good for getting a particular answer from an individual child, but we need to know for sure that the child will be able to answer and not made to look silly. Again, leading questions can move children towards a personal response to what they have discovered.

Now practise your question technique by:

Absorbing this summary of the types of question that may help children learn about the Bible.

Selecting another Bible passage and writing down as many of each type of question as you can.

Writing down (or getting another group leader or parent to write down) the kind of answers you might expect children to give to your questions.

Chapter Seven

'IT DOESN'T ALWAYS MEAN WHAT IT SAYS'

ROOT PROBLEM

Once, there were two worried twelve-year-olds, Christopher and Stephen . . .

Chris says, 'I like reading the Bible but there's one verse I don't understand. It's Proverbs 20:10 – "The Lord hates people who use dishonest weights and measures." I thought God loved everyone*!'*

We struggle to give him a satisfying answer. Ah, well, yes, of course you're right. God does love everyone, but no doubt you have heard the story of the mother who shouted at her children, 'How many millions of times have I told you not to exaggerate!' We exaggerate all the time, don't we? In writing and speaking, exaggeration (or 'hyperbole') is used to make a point very strongly. When Solomon wrote Proverbs 20:10, he wanted to use very strong language so that people would listen and stop cheating each other with dishonest weights and measures. What he meant, of course, was 'God hates cheating', but saying it like that wouldn't have had the same impact.

So, we have a problem. Chris is most familiar with the Bible stories in which what he reads is exactly what happens. Maybe he has never before come across Proverbs, where language is used in a different way, and no one proverb by itself gives the complete picture of what it is talking about. Proverbs were written to be memorable, to make an immediate, lasting impression on the behaviour of those reading or hearing them. Telling people God hated them would definitely have stuck in their minds!

And what about Stephen?

'There's a part of the Bible that I don't understand at all, except I do know it's about the end of the world. It's Revelation 14:1–5.

Verse 1 says, "Then I looked, and there was the Lamb standing on Mount Zion; with him were 144,000 people who have his name and his Father's name written on their foreheads." Does this mean there'll only be 144,000 people in heaven? And if so, will they all be Jews?'

Once again we are put on the spot. Ah, well, yes, you have picked a tough bit there! You need to read Revelation 5: 9–10 and 7: 1–8 with these verses to make the best sense of them. They show that the 144,000 are made up from all the twelve tribes of Israel, but that God's chosen people will come from 'every tribe and language and people and nation'. I know the words here say '144,000 ' but the number actually has a special meaning. It is 'symbolic' – it means all God's chosen people, who were originally the Jews (from the twelve tribes of Israel) but who now include all those who trust in Jesus.

So we have another problem. Revelation is *visionary* writing in which the writer pictured the things to come in the way he saw and understood them at the time he was writing. Sometimes the written detail has to be understood as poetic language, describing something even more real than the words could say. Stephen easily grasps story, vision and poetry when he meets them in other places, but somehow adults have persuaded him that the words on the Bible's pages mean exactly what they say.

There are many different kinds of writing in the Bible, but we often treat the biblical text in a way that suggests it is all basically the same, all to be understood in the same way. Yet God has chosen to communicate with us in a rich variety of ways.

The stories and poems of the Bible achieve their devotional purpose whenever they reinforce a reader's general sense of the reality of God, or produce an awareness of what is moral or immoral, or influence a person's estimate of what is valuable and worthless. We are affected by more than ideas when we read literature, though, of course, ideas are part of the total experience. We read literature not primarily to acquire information but to contemplate experience and reality as a way of understanding them better. One of the rewards of reading literature, including the Bible, is that our own experience and beliefs are given shape and expression. (From *How to Read The Bible as Literature* by Leland Ryken.)

Of course, there is much more to the Bible than stories and poems! The sooner we help children to appreciate this, the sooner we will help them get rid of some damaging ideas that come from only hearing Bible stories with moral applications bolted onto the end of them, ideas like . . .

'The Bible is more boring than any other book because all it does is tell us how to behave all the time.'

'What happens in the Bible belongs to a world far away and a long, long time ago.'

'Now we know all the Bible stories, we've "done" the Bible and can get on to something more interesting and "grown-up".'

'What God does with other people is more real and more important than what he does with us.'

GROWING TREES
Before we begin to enjoy the richness of the Bible's different kinds of writing, we need to make sure that our children can handle the Bible as a whole book for themselves. Bible Activity 3 'Place Setter' and Bible Activity 4 'WayFinder' will help you do this.

At this point, maybe you're thinking, 'Uh-oh, ours don't "do" books. They can't read very well, or at least they choose not to. Getting them to handle any book would be like getting next door's dog to sing the Hallelujah Chorus!'

Well, I hope that even the most 'reluctant' reader can be encouraged to handle the Bible in some way and for some purpose before too long. Let's not abandon books altogether! Understanding what is in the Bible and how it 'works' is going to help them understand better the bits they do hear anyway. Bible Activity 6 'Not Just Words' suggests ways of helping those who are not happy with reading.

The Bible as a library of books

Now what kind of reading materials do I have at home? Ah, my wife Sue has started to put our books into some kind of order. What's this? My least favourite book, but one I couldn't do without – The Reader's Digest Repair Manual. *Yawn, what a bore!*

> 'Shut off the water supply and open the tap or valve fully. Fit waste plug in sink. Protect shield with rag and remove it with a spanner.'

So why do I need a spanner to remove the rag? Oh well, better do as it says – one day.

Look, here are those Jeffrey Archer stories, A Twist in the Tale. *I never finished those . . .*

> 'Christopher and Margaret Roberts always spent their summer holiday as far away from England as they could possibly afford. However, as Christopher was the classics master at St Cuthbert's, a small preparatory school just north of Yeovil, and Margaret was the school matron, their experience of four of the five continents was largely confined to periodicals such as National Geographic *magazine . . .'*

That can go beside the bed – maybe I'll actually finish it if it stares me in the face every night.

Ah, this is better – something in small, funny chunks that isn't too demanding. Spike Milligan's Startling Verse for All the Family . . .

> 'My grandad's old
> And lost his hair
> And that's why flies
> Are landing there.'

We must have some greater poetry in the house than that! – Yes, Gerard Manley Hopkins' Poems and Prose:

> 'Summer ends now; now, barbarous in beauty, the stooks rise
> Around; up above, what wind-walks! What lovely behaviour
> Of silk-sack clouds! has wilder, wilful-wavier

Meal-drift moulded ever and melted across the skies? . . .

Ah, yes, I remember summer. We had one once.

Now who's that on the phone just as I'm about to sink into an armchair with the local paper?

'Yes? . . . Oh, hello there . . . Next week? Hold on, I'll just grab my diary . . . Let me see . . . Monday is our admin meeting at work. Then I'm in Nottingham for a training event, so can't do anything there. Tuesday I'm in the office, but in a meeting all morning. Wednesday is Anna's birthday, so I've got the day off to help with the party − except − Groan! There's a meeting I simply must go to right in the middle of Wednesday . . . Sorry, you don't need to hear all this. Look, Thursday is the first space I have. Four o'clock at your place? . . . OK, see you then. Bye!'

Where would I be without my diary? My whole life written up in brief for easy reference!

Ah, the Prince of Wales seems to be telling it as it is in The National Trust Magazine:

> 'The ancient idea that mankind has a responsibility for the stewardship of the natural world, and hence of the countryside, may not be particularly fashionable, but I believe it lies at the heart of the concept of sustainability which has currently received so much attention. We will only achieve sustainability by looking at the long-term consequences of our actions, recognising that natural systems have finite limits . . .'

More of that later too! Now where's that paper gone? Right, let's have a look at the TV programmes . . .

> '6.00 News
> 6.30 Midlands Today
> 7.00 This is Your Life
> 7.30 As Time Goes By
> 8.00 How Do They Do That?
> 8.45 Points of View
> 9.00 News
> 9.30 Alas Smith and Jones . . .'

Hmm . . . it might be an evening to snuggle up with a good book!

What's this stuffed under the chair? Terry Waite's Taken on Trust.
*Ah, Sue must be into this. Wait a minute. There's a letter in here
keeping her place.*

> 'Dear Terry and Sue,
> I do hope this finds you in the best of health and enjoying
> life to the full. I trust the family is well. Last time I wrote
> was, I think, just after my birthday . . .'

*I don't remember seeing that before . . . Oh well, back to Terry
Waite.*

> 'I have lost track of the days. It's probably Tuesday, but I
> can't be sure. One day is very much the same as another.
> Bread and lebne for breakfast, one quick visit to the bathroom,
> and then twenty-three hours and fifty minutes lying in the
> corner with nothing but my thoughts. I live on sandwiches
> and two cups of tea a day. It's enough. The guard is
> watching an Arabic programme on television. Someone taps
> on the apartment door, and I can hear voices in the hallway.
> Visitors arouse my fear. Several people enter the room. I
> recognize the old man with the cold and the man in the
> suit . . .'

*Brilliant! I really must start this when Sue has finished with it.
But maybe something a bit lighter and shorter for this evening . . .
Terry Pratchett's stuff is fairly escapist. Well, at least he helps us to
see life from another angle. What does the blurb say on the cover of*
Truckers?

> 'To the thousands of tiny nomes who live under the floor
> boards of a large department store, there is no Outside.
> Things like Day and Night, Sun and Rain are just daft old
> legends.
>   Then a devastating piece of news shatters their existence:
> the Store — their whole world — is to be demolished. And it's
> up to Masklin, one of the last nomes to come into the Store,
> to mastermind an unbelievable escape plan that will take
> all the nomes into the dangers of the great Outside . . .'

That's more like it. I'll catch up with you later! . . .

Why do we need all these different sorts of writing?

Because they help us to survive, to enjoy what other people have created, to do things we have never done before, to know what is going on in the world, to understand and express ourselves better, to see things from other people's points of view, to spread our lives out before ourselves and other people at a glance, to dream dreams of what life could be like, somehow to enrich our life and get more out of it.

Why are there so many different sorts of writing in the Bible? To help us to survive, to enjoy what other people have created, to do things we have never done before, to know what is going on in the world, to understand and express ourselves better, to see things from other people's points of view, to spread our lives out before ourselves and other people at a glance, to dream dreams of what life could be like, somehow to enrich our life and to get more out of it . . .

And to know God. Yes, above all, to know God.

But we can't appreciate the different kinds of Bible literature just by reading about them. Let's actually *immerse* ourselves in them. Once we get 'under their skin' ourselves, we will be able to see more clearly how to get 'under their skin' with children.

Now, don't forget – this is a workbook above all. So grab yourself a pencil and get ready to write.

∾ Plans for Growth ∾

Plan 1
On the following pages are a series of exercises that will help you take a closer look at each of the different types of Bible writing. Try doing one exercise each day – you may end up with literary indigestion if you try them all at one go!

• STORIES AND HISTORIES

1 Kings 8:1–13

Setting the scene:
King Solomon has finished building the Temple in Jerusalem to the very highest specification. Only the best is good enough for God.

¹Then King Solomon summoned all the leaders of the tribes and clans of Israel to come to him in Jerusalem in order to take the Lord's Covenant Box from Zion, David's city, to the Temple. ²They all assembled during the Festival of Shelters in the seventh month, in the month of Ethanim. ³When all the leaders had gathered, the priests lifted the Covenant Box ⁴and carried it to the Temple. The Levites and the priests also moved the Tent of the Lord's presence and all its equipment to the Temple. ⁵King Solomon and all the people of Israel assembled in front of the Covenant Box and sacrificed a large number of sheep and cattle – too many to count. ⁶Then the priests carried the Covenant Box into the Temple and put it in the Most Holy Place, beneath the winged creatures. ⁷Their outstretched wings covered the box and the poles it was carried by. ⁸The ends of the poles could be seen by anyone standing directly in front of the Most Holy Place, but from nowhere else. (The poles are still there today.) ⁹There was nothing inside the Covenant Box except the two stone tablets which Moses had placed there at Mount Sinai, when the Lord made a covenant with the people of Israel as they were coming out of Egypt.
¹⁰As the priests were leaving the Temple, it was suddenly filled with a cloud ¹¹shining with the dazzling light of the Lord's presence, and they could not go back in to perform their duties. ¹²Then Solomon prayed:
'You, Lord, have placed the sun in the sky,
    yet you have chosen to live in clouds and darkness.
¹³Now I have built a majestic temple for you,
    a place for you to live in for ever.'

Pray that you will be receptive to what God is doing and to what he wants to say to you through these verses.

Read the verses through, underlining all the details that you think add colour to this episode.

Think about why the writer might have included so much detail about where things happened and where people were standing.

Write in the margins all you can discover from the verses about Solomon, the priests and the crowd of tribal leaders. Link your comments to part of the text with a pencil line.

What does Solomon actually do and say?

What mood does the writer generate?

Using a pencil to circle the appropriate verses, divide them into 'scenes' as if these episodes were a film. Visualise how the story would unfold scene by scene if you were watching a film.

What changes are there between the beginning and the end of the story?

If you were taking part in this episode, who and where would you be?

Read the verses again, experiencing everything from your new viewpoint.

What do you think God is doing here? What is the story about?

How would you like to respond to God in the light of what you have experienced?

• LAWS

Deuteronomy 23:15–25

Setting the scene:

After God rescued the Israelites from slavery in Egypt, he gave them over 600 laws. These were designed to help them become a strong nation and to live in a way that fitted with their being God's people. The laws would ensure that the life of the Israelites reflected what God was like to the people around them, showing their special relationship with him and their loyalty to him.

[15]'If a slave runs away from his or her owner and comes to you for protection, do not send them back. [16]They may live in any of your towns that they choose, and you are not to treat them harshly.

[17]'No Israelite, man or woman, is to become a temple prostitute. [18]Also, no money earned in this way may be brought into the house of the Lord your God in fulfilment of a vow. The Lord hates temple prostitutes.

[19]'When you lend money or food or anything else to a fellow–

Israelite, do not charge him interest. [20]You may charge interest on what you lend to a foreigner, but not on what you lend to a fellow-Israelite. Obey this rule, and the Lord your God will bless everything you do in the land that you are going to occupy.

[21]'When you make a vow to the Lord your God, do not put off doing what you promised; the Lord will hold you to your vow, and it is a sin not to keep it. [22]It is no sin not to make a vow to the Lord, [23]but if you make one voluntarily, be sure that you keep it.

[24]'When you walk along a path in someone else's vineyard, you may eat all the grapes you want, but you must not carry any away in a container. [25]When you walk along a path in someone else's cornfield, you may eat all the corn you can pull off with your hands, but you must not cut any corn with a sickle.'

Pray that you will appreciate more fully God's care for people and catch a glimpse of his holiness, his high standards of righteousness and his hatred of wrong.

Look at each law one by one. How would keeping them bring the Israelites, in the long run, greater release rather than restriction?

Decide whether the laws are to do with the Israelites' civil life or their worship. Do these laws encourage us to think about our treatment of others, or to consider our worship of God? Or are these two aspects inextricably linked in some way?

What do the laws tell us about God and about the kind of things he loves and hates?

These laws are examples for us to see what it meant in those days to be loyal to God. What kind of standard do they set?

What is the 'spirit' of these laws, or the message or principle behind them, that we can recognise from Jesus' teaching and from other parts of the New Testament?

What might this 'spirit of the law' mean for our own lives? We don't need to keep the same rules, but we do need to demonstrate, distinctively and visibly, that we belong to God by the way we live.

Tell God how humble it makes you feel (if it does) when you realise how far short of his standards you fall. We don't deserve to belong to him. We simply can't meet his high standards of righteousness by ourselves. But thank him for sending Jesus to die so that our falling-short need not count against us, and so that we can be accepted by God as holy people.

• PROVERBS AND WISDOM

Proverbs 18:1–24

Setting the scene:
These proverbs about how we should live are reckoned to have been written by King Solomon. True wisdom, says Solomon, is to live in a right relationship with God. The proverbs show how the wise, God-fearing person will live day by day.

Only occasionally do proverbs follow on logically one from another, so don't expect a coherent theme through this chapter. Sometimes odd proverbs on their own seem to say strange and inappropriate things when compared with the teaching of Jesus and the rest of the New Testament. So it is advisable to gather together all the proverbs on a particular subject (eg friendship) before stating categorically what you believe Solomon says on the subject, and then weigh this against what the rest of the Bible says.

¹People who do not get along with others are interested only in themselves; they will disagree with what everyone else knows is right.

²A fool does not care whether he understands a thing or not; all he wants to do is to show how clever he is.

³Sin and shame go together. Lose your honour, and you will get scorn in its place.

⁴A person's words can be a source of wisdom, deep as the ocean, fresh as a flowing stream.

⁵It is not right to favour the guilty and prevent the innocent from receiving justice.

⁶When some fool starts an argument, he is asking for a beating.

⁷When a fool speaks, he is ruining himself; he gets caught in the trap of his own words.

⁸Gossip is so tasty – how we love to swallow it!

⁹A lazy person is as bad as someone who is destructive.

¹⁰The Lord is like a strong tower, where the righteous can

go and be safe. [11]Rich people, however, imagine that their wealth protects them like high, strong walls round a city.

[12]No one is respected unless he is humble; arrogant people are on the way to ruin.

[13]Listen before you answer. If you don't, you are being stupid and insulting.

[14]Your will to live can sustain you when you are sick, but if you lose it, your last hope is gone.

[15]Intelligent people are always eager and ready to learn.

[16]Do you want to meet an important person? Take him a gift and it will be easy.

[17]The first to speak in court always seems right until his opponent begins to question him.

[18]If two powerful men are opposing each other in court, casting lots can settle the issue.

[19]Help your relatives and they will protect you like a strong city wall, but if you quarrel with them, they will close their doors to you.

[20]You will have to live with the consequences of everything you say. [21]What you say can preserve life or destroy it; so you must accept the consequences of your words.

[22]Find a wife and you find a good thing; it shows that the Lord is good to you.

[23]When the poor speak, they have to beg politely, but when the rich answer, they are rude.

[24]Some friendships do not last, but some friends are more loyal than brothers.

Pray that the areas of your life which need special attention will 'leap out' at you during your exploration of these proverbs.

Read the whole passage slowly, picturing the different scenes one at a time in your mind.

Sketch one or two of them as cartoons in the margin or write one or two key words to show what each is about, if you like.

Life is full of fast-and-furious experiences one after the other like this. Read the proverbs again, thinking of a real-life example of what each one says. Do any examples seem to go against what you already know pleases God according to the rest of the Bible?

Underline any proverbs that seem to ring bells with you. These may have special importance for you just now. Pray about what they say.

• POETRY AND SONG

Psalm 19:1–14

Setting the scene:
Psalms help us to remember how God works and to worship him. This one reminds us that God communicates wonderfully through both creation and his written word.

¹How clearly the sky reveals God's glory!
How plainly it shows what he has done!
²Each day announces it to the following day;
    each night repeats it to the next.
³No speech or words are used,
    no sound is heard;
⁴yet their message goes out to all the world
    and is heard to the ends of the earth.
God made a home in the sky for the sun;
⁵ it comes out in the morning like a happy bridegroom,
    like an athlete eager to run a race.
⁶It starts at one end of the sky
    and goes across to the other.
    Nothing can hide from its heat.

⁷The law of the Lord is perfect;
    it gives new strength.
The commands of the Lord are trustworthy,
    giving wisdom to those who lack it.
⁸The laws of the Lord are right,
    and those who obey them are happy.
The commands of the Lord are just
    and give understanding to the mind.
⁹Reverence for the Lord is good;
    it will continue for ever.
The judgements of the Lord are just;
    they are always fair.
¹⁰They are more desirable than the finest gold;
    they are sweeter than the purest honey.
¹¹They give knowledge to me, your servant;
    I am rewarded for obeying them.

¹²No one can see his own errors;
    deliver me, Lord, from hidden faults!
¹³Keep me safe, also, from wilful sins;
    don't let them rule over me.
Then I shall be perfect
    and free from the evil of sin.

¹⁴May my words and my thoughts be acceptable to you,
   O Lord, my refuge and my redeemer!

Pray that you will allow the poetry of this psalm to broaden
your knowledge of God and to move you to worship.

Read the psalm slowly, trying to picture everything in your
mind's eye. Try also to sense the emotion in the poet's
words.

Underline all the comparisons or things that aren't literally
true, eg 'like a happy bridegroom', or 'their message goes
out to all the world'. Against each, write what you think
it means. Give as many possibilities as you can.

Look for parallelism, and mark these verses like this: | |.
'Parallelism' consists of two or more lines that use different
words to describe the same thing with a similar kind of
sentence. What do you think the poet is stressing each
time?

So what is the poet telling us about God, his creation and
his written word?

Read the whole psalm again, this time pausing to respond
to God at any point where you are moved by what you
are reading.

• PROPHECY

Hosea 14:1–9

Setting the scene:

Hosea spoke God's word to the people of the northern
kingdom of Israel around 734 BC. He warned them that,
because of their disobedience and unfaithfulness towards
God, they would be overrun by Assyria. The sad things that
happened to Hosea, particularly when his wife deserted him,
served to illustrate how God felt about the people of Israel
turning their backs on him and worshipping idols. However,
God's love is stronger than anything.

After constant pleading with Israel to change her ways,
Hosea finally gives the people words of repentance to say,
and the promise of God's forgiveness. We know from history

that the people refused to take notice of Hosea, and Israel *was* overrun by the Assyrians.

¹Return to the Lord your God, people of Israel. Your sin has made you stumble and fall. ²Return to the Lord, and let this prayer be your offering to him: 'Forgive all our sins and accept our prayer, and we will praise you as we have promised. ³Assyria can never save us, and the war horses cannot protect us. We will never again say to our idols that they are our God. O Lord, you show mercy to those who have no one else to turn to.'

⁴The Lord says,
'I will bring my people back to me.
I will love them with all my heart;
    no longer am I angry with them.
⁵I will be to the people of Israel
    like rain in a dry land.
They will blossom like flowers;
    they will be firmly rooted
    like the trees of Lebanon.
⁶They will be alive with new growth,
    and beautiful like olive trees.
They will be fragrant
    like the cedars of Lebanon.
⁷Once again they will live under my protection.
They will grow corn
    and be fruitful like a vineyard.
    They will be as famous as the wine of Lebanon.
⁸The people of Israel will have nothing more to do
    with idols;
    I will answer their prayers and take care of them;
Like an evergreen tree I will shelter them;
    I am the source of all their blessings.'

⁹May those who are wise understand what is written here, and may they take it to heart. The Lord's ways are right, and righteous people live by following them, but sinners stumble and fall because they ignore them.

Pray that the prophet's words will draw you back to God. Read the verses slowly, preferably aloud, looking carefully for what they say about the wrong in the lives of God's people. What does God want and what doesn't he want? In the margin, jot down any thoughts that come to mind.

Read the verses aloud again, focusing this time on what they say about the depths of God's love for his people.

Underline all the images that Hosea uses – descriptive words or phrases that vividly convey meaning without being literally true. In the space, note down what you think each image might be suggesting.

Does God say the same thing twice anywhere, though perhaps using different words or images?

What God wanted and didn't want for Israel is, in general terms, what he wants and doesn't want for us. If we obey him – loving him by faith in Christ and living to please him as best we know how from the Bible – we will be blessed, though not necessarily with Old Testament style prosperity. What do you think these verses say about your own life? How do they suggest you might be drawn back to God?

Pray that you will not ignore Hosea's words in the way that Israel did.

• GOSPEL EPISODE

Mark 3:1–6

Setting the scene:
In the first century AD, Christians were persecuted, arrested and sometimes executed for their faith. If Peter the apostle were killed in this way, how would the good news about who Jesus was, what he came to do and what he taught, be handed on reliably to new Christians? Scholars think that John Mark decided to write down Peter's words, and the result was Mark's Gospel.

In the first half of the Gospel, Mark tells of many incidents which show that Jesus is the Son of God.

¹Then Jesus went back to the synagogue, where there was a man who had a paralysed hand. ²Some people were there who wanted to accuse Jesus of doing wrong; so they watched him

closely to see whether he would heal the man on the Sabbath.
³Jesus said to the man, 'Come up here to the front.' ⁴Then he
asked the people, 'What does our Law allow us to do on the
Sabbath? To help or to harm? To save a man's life or to
destroy it?'

But they did not say a thing. ⁵Jesus was angry as he looked
round at them, but at the same time he felt sorry for them,
because they were so stubborn and wrong. Then he said to the
man, 'Stretch our your hand.' He stretched out his hand, and
it became well again. ⁶So the Pharisees left the synagogue
and met at once with some members of Herod's party, and
they made plans to kill Jesus.

Pray that your reading of these verses will help you to meet
Jesus in a new way and be amazed by him.

In your Bible, notice what happens immediately before and
after these verses.

Read through the verses slowly. Think what they seem most
naturally to be about.

Ask yourself why this episode is written at this point in
Mark's Gospel. How do you think it might have helped
those who read or heard these words originally?

Go through this episode, chopping it into 'scenes' by drawing
circles round verses with a pencil as you did before.
Imagine you are making a TV drama and want to mark
where you will change the camera shot.

Mark the scenes 'D' to show if they are distant shots, 'C' if
they are close-ups, or 'CS' if they are crowd scenes.

How would you show the mounting tension between Jesus
and the Pharisees?

Put yourself in the episode as someone who meets Jesus on
this occasion. Who would you like to be? Relive the
episode as that person.

What one question would you like to ask Jesus while all this
is happening? Turn your question into prayer to him.

● LETTER/EPISTLE

1 Peter 4:7–11

Setting the scene:
Before you begin, discover for yourself who this letter was

written by, to whom it is addressed and what their situation was at the time. Read up as much background detail of 1 Peter as you can. A Bible handbook or the introduction to a commentary will help without giving too much detail.

> [7]The end of all things is near. You must be self-controlled and alert, to be able to pray. [8]Above everything, love one another earnestly, because love covers over many sins. [9]Open your homes to each other without complaining. [10]Each one, as a good manager of God's different gifts, must use for the good of others the special gift he has received from God. [11]Whoever preaches must preach God's messages; whoever serves must serve with the strength that God gives him, so that in all things praise may be given to God through Jesus Christ, to whom belong the glory and power for ever and ever. Amen.

Pray that something in these verses will help to change an attitude or a pattern of behaviour that you have.

In the *Good News Bible*, read the whole of 1 Peter right through. It shouldn't take you longer than about ten minutes.

Note down a few words in the margins of this page to show what the flow of argument is in the letter as a whole.

So how does this part of the letter fit into the whole? If Peter were reading 1 Peter 4:7–11 out loud, what tone of voice do you think he would use? Read it aloud in that way, if you dare!

Go back to your commentary to study these four verses in depth. How do you think they relate to your own life just now? Talk to God about this.

• VISIONARY/APOCALYPTIC WRITING

Revelation 4:1–11

Setting the scene:

One of the New Testament books that wasn't written by Paul is Revelation. It was probably written about sixty years after Jesus died, at a time when Christians were being persecuted and were wondering if this was the end for God's people. The Romans wanted them to worship the emperor and say 'Caesar is Lord!' rather than 'Jesus is Lord!' A church leader called John refused and ʋas exiled to the tiny Greek island of Patmos. There God gave him a vision, which is recorded in the book of Revelation. After chapter 3, Revelation uses picture-language. Images 'reveal' to us a little of what was really happening during the first-century persecution, and what will happen in the future. The impact of the pictures should encourage us – as it would have the first-century Christians – to keep going when life is hard and we are in danger.

[1]At this point I had another vision and saw an open door in heaven. And the voice that sounded like a trumpet, which I had heard speaking to me before, said, 'Come up here, and I will show you what must happen after this.' [2]At once the Spirit took control of me. There in heaven was a throne with someone sitting on it. [3]His face gleamed like such precious stones as jasper and carnelian, and all round the throne there was a rainbow the colour of an emerald. [4]In a circle round the throne were twenty-four other thrones, on which were seated twenty-four elders dressed in white and wearing crowns of gold. [5]From the throne came flashes of lightning, rumblings, and peals of thunder. In front of the throne seven lighted torches were burning, which are the seven spirits of God. [6]Also in front of the throne there was what looked like a sea of glass, clear as crystal.

Surrounding the throne on each of its sides, were four living creatures covered with eyes in front and behind. [7]The first one looked like a lion; the second looked like a bull; the third had a face like a human face; and the fourth looked like an eagle in flight. [8]Each one of the four living creatures had six wings, and they were covered with eyes, inside and out. Day and night they never stop singing:

'Holy, holy, holy, is the Lord God Almighty,
   who was, who is, and who is to come.'

[9]The four living creatures sing songs of glory and honour and thanks to the one who sits on the throne, who lives for ever and ever. When they do so, [10]the twenty-four elders fall down before the one who sits on the throne, and worship him who lives for ever and ever. They throw their crowns down in front of the throne and say:

[11]'Our Lord and God! You are worthy
   to receive glory, honour, and power.
For you created all things.
   and by your will they were given existence and life.'

Pray that God will give you hope and encouragement through these verses.

Read as much of the book of Revelation as you can. It should only take about thirty minutes. Get ready to travel to a new level of reality!

Read the verses printed above as slowly as you can, imagining each scene as it happens. The images don't necessarily flow together – they are more like a series of cartoon-strip pictures, slightly disjointed and with a constantly changing focus. Simply try to get the feel of what's going on.

Imagine you are explaining to a child what is in these verses. It is not a story to tell, more like a picture to describe.

See if you can find the words to describe where the scenes take place, who the main characters are, what they do and what happens in the end.

Think about any situation that is currently making you fearful or threatening your faith. Talk to God honestly about it.

If you haven't done so already, see 'the one on the throne' as Jesus. As you read the verses once more, think of Jesus as the one who is all-powerful and ultimately in control. How do you feel now about the situation you have just prayed about?

Finally, join the crowds in heaven, worshipping Christ with the words of verses 8b and 11.

Now that you have enjoyed each type of biblical writing for yourself, you may begin to see how you could adapt each kind of approach for use with children. Before you start your preparation, always think, 'What kind of writing is this?'

Old or New Testament stories and histories

Children will probably find a narrative approach best, and this will do justice to the way God has chosen to communicate the truth in the Bible. You tell or retell the Bible story, share true stories about yourself and others; the children see the story on video or listen to it on tape, then tell part of their own life story, entering into the Bible story by their imaginations; then they draw, write, tell or act out a version of the story, or invent their own, to say the same thing about God. In fact, try any way of using stories without spending too much time dissecting them and analysing each of the components.

Old Testament laws

Count on your children's curiosity to get into the cultural and historical background. This is vital for any understanding of what God was getting at! Never give the impression that God wants us to obey these rules unless this is made clear in Jesus' teaching or in other places in the New Testament. Instead, look for the message behind the laws, or for the 'spirit of the law', and what this shows us about God's love and justice. Try to 'paint pictures' of what life was like then under these laws (perhaps through role-play), and of what life is like now as we try to live according to the standards that Jesus taught. Always show how keeping God's laws then and now means the best kind of life for everyone.

Proverb and other wisdom writing

Illustrate this kind of writing with very down-to-earth situations that the children might find themselves in, but don't expect all children to latch onto all proverbs equally. Some proverbs will be more memorable and mean more for some than others. Many proverbs are humorous, so use humour or, better still, get the children to use theirs. Short snippets of wisdom need a bitty, but vivid approach if they are to stick in the mind. Search in other chapters of Proverbs for advice on the same subject.

Poetry and song

Expect children to be able to listen to poems being read and to enjoy them. They may have experienced poetry at school and know how to handle it. Invite them to express their feelings – poetry works primarily at an emotional level. Ask the children to do their own creative activity in response to the poetry, and to write their own poems about their own lives using the same theme as the biblical material. Poetry is creative expression; our exploration of it with children should involve that too!

Prophecy

You will have a lot of work to do before exploring prophetic writing with children, but this is no reason to avoid it! Prophecy can give children a clear insight into what God is like. First, use Bible dictionaries, commentaries and handbooks yourself in order to grasp the answers to the 'Who?' 'To whom?' 'Where?' 'When?'and 'Why?' questions of the prophecy.

Because prophecy is 'telling it as it is', you will have to think carefully about how your children actually *hear* the words you are presenting, how they will see vividly the historical context of the words, how they will explore the images in the prophecy (as dramatically as possible!), and how they will answer our big questions about God:

Who does this part of the Bible tell us God is, directly in the words or because of the kinds of things he is doing or saying?

What is God like in this passage?

What has he done? Or what is he doing now? Or what *will* he do?

What does God want?

What doesn't he want?

What might it be like to live with this God?

Gospel episodes

Remember that the Gospels are an invitation to meet Jesus and to see God in him. As Jesus met, taught and healed many people *then*, so he wants to meet, teach and heal us *now*. Putting ourselves in the shoes of the people in the crowd or the individuals who met Jesus will help his words and actions come home to us.

Letters/Epistles

Explore all that happens in and around Bible letters. They were written thoughtfully, sent, carried, received, opened, read out loud or silently. (New Testament letters would probably have been read aloud to the churches they were written to.) Someone probably replied to them and kept them because they were special. Start exploring Bible letters by actually using letters you have sent or received, but keep in mind that biblical epistles were more like 'portable' sermons than chatty, personal news.

Visonary/Apocalyptic writing
This kind of writing originated as something that someone saw in a particular way, so try using a visual approach. An image is more likely to be remembered (for example, Ezekiel's dry bones becoming living bodies), and it is in the image that the truth is found.

> Bible Activity 12 'Gotta Get a Message to You' (page 165) suggests ways of exploring each kind of Bible writing with children.

Plan 2

This activity should be fairly relaxing! What is missing in your life which could be represented by one of the different kinds of Bible literature? You may like to choose one or more of the following activities. And try to find a way of enjoying the experience if you wouldn't normally!

Stories and histories
Watch a Christian video with a strong story-line, or curl up with a Christian biography or autobiography.

Laws
Think of some of the rules you impose on your own children or the children in your group. Are they good rules? Are they making life better for everyone, or restricting the children in an unhelpful or even damaging way?

Proverbs and other wisdom writing
Find time to listen to an old person talking about his or her faith.

Poetry and song
Ask a friend or your spouse to read some Christian poetry aloud to you.

Prophecy
Listen to a rousing sermon on tape.

Short bursts of good news
Listen to a Christian radio station or read a Christian newspaper, picking out the good news especially.

Letter
Write someone an encouraging letter, or enjoy reading an encouraging letter you have received recently from a Christian friend.

Vision
Dream a few dreams about your church. What images could you use to describe what it is now and what you would like it to be?

Plan 3
Invite some children to tell you what they are reading and writing at school. What do they do with stories and poems, for instance? Look at their school books, if they will let you and if they have any!

Chapter Eight

'BIBLE STORIES ARE BAD NEWS'

ROOT PROBLEM

During my childhood and teenage years, the real-life story of Moses receiving the Ten Commandments always made my heart sink. This, I felt, was God on a bad day. A list of dos and don'ts for his people seemed like a desperate measure and didn't fit at all with my image of a dynamic, never-failing, universe-creating, all-loving God. Also, I knew exactly what was coming. We were going to plough through the Commandments one at a time and, of course, I would fail at just about all of them (again!). Then, to make matters worse, my group leader would bring Jesus into the picture and stretch the definitions of, say, murder and adultery to include even unsavoury thoughts as well. Groan – I didn't stand a chance!

Of course, my group leaders were right to show how my life didn't match up to God's standards. (I had a fair idea anyway that this might be the case, him being amazing and God and perfect and everything, and me not being any of those things.) But the trouble was, they were only giving me *half* the story, and that is what wasn't fair about our look at Exodus chapter 20.

You see, I don't recall hearing about the thunder and lightning, the thick black cloud that appeared on Mount Sinai, the loud trumpet blast, the sheer terror of the people at the thought of God being so close, God's call to Moses, and Moses' long climb up Sinai. And, all the while, the trumpet sounding louder and louder . . . I don't remember hearing that God gave the Ten Commandments to his people because he cared passionately about them; because he wanted them to demonstrate his character to the rest of the world; because he wanted to give them boundaries within which they could have tremendous freedom and responsibility for a life of love and respect – 'Just follow these rules, then live how you like!' Even though they were restrictions on the Israelites' way of life, the Commandments were ultimately intended for freedom – to help the Israelites live the very best kind of life. But they felt more like a cage to me.

The *whole* story would have filled me with a far greater sense of awe, of God's holiness and of my unworthiness. With a 'rules checklist' and nothing else, I was getting all the moral standards but no clearer image of the God who set the standards. For some reason, someone somewhere wanted to change my behaviour as soon as possible, so that person put the focus on one place (the rules) rather than on two places (God *and* the rules). I was cheated out of the story that went with the rules, so that I felt crushed, not liberated into a life that would please God. Other Bible stories also ended up like that for me – they were bad news.

Steve stood up in front of the group and tried to get their attention. Outside it was bucketing down with rain. The children had arrived as high as kites and soaking wet. The pile of coats steamed gently in the corner.

To get things started, Steve organised a game which involved the children buzzing round the walls as fast as they could, picking up clues about who the main character was to be in the day's Bible story. They had to come and whisper the answer in his ear as soon as they thought they knew, and he would tell them if they were right or not. If they were wrong, they had to carry on picking up clues. If they were right, they could sit on the mat in the middle and thump each other. Well, Steve didn't actually suggest they thumped each other – they just did!

When there was only one bedraggled girl left leaning hopelessly against the wall, pretending still to be working out the answer, Steve thought it was time to put her out of her misery and get into the Bible story itself. Tanya sat down, deflated. Steve began.

'Hello! (Hello, Steve!) Now, just about all of you guessed who today's story is about, didn't you? (Yes!) Never mind if you didn't, Tanya. You'll soon find out where you went wrong. Are you all ready? (Yes!) Good. Here we go.

'Thomas came crashing in through the front door. He was breathless. He had run all the way down from the hills. He was so excited

about what had happened. He'd been with Jesus all day. Perhaps you could all be a bit more excited about Jesus than you usually are.

'Thomas blurted out, *"Listen, Mum. I know I should have been home an hour ago, but the most amazing thing has just happened. I've been out in the hills listening to Jesus. There were thousands of us! Like a load of sheep we were, all following him around . . . Well, I knew it was getting late, Mum — we all did. But we just didn't want to go home."* Have you ever been really naughty and stayed out later than you should have? I bet you have!

' *"Wow, the way Jesus talks and the things he says — Mum, he's the best!"* Thomas went on. *"Anyway, we were all getting really hungry when some bloke came and tapped me on the shoulder and said, "'Ere, sonny. Give us your bread and fish. The Master wants them." So I did. Jesus took my whole lunch and . . . and somehow made enough food from it for everyone. Everyone had a bellyful! And there was tons left over too! Tons!"*

'That's where today's Bible story ends, and this is what it's about. You must give Jesus everything you've got, just like Thomas did. Because you're naturally sinful, you want to keep everything for yourself. But Jesus wants your time, your money, your love, the TV in your bedroom . . . Let's ask Jesus now to make you all more generous.'

Aaargh! There it is — one spoilt, devalued, abused Bible story, and one spoilt, devalued, abused group of children. Steve knows that the Bible challenges our children's way of life as well as our own, but he has let his own desire for 'progress' in the children completely overrule what this part of the Bible is actually saying. As Larry Richards says in *Talkable Bible Stories*:

> You and I are not to use the Bible to club a child, or to impose demands that he or she conform. We are to use Bible stories . . . as a doorway to hope rather than as a nagging demand for change.

GROWING TREES

Stories fascinate — they draw children and adults irresistibly into the worlds they create. They are rich: they feed the imagination with colour, movement, sound and scents; they provide heroes to side with and villains to loathe; they raise questions and hint at answers. Everyone loves a story.

Much of an adult's day and most of a child's day is filled with stories — news reports at the breakfast table, computer games, films, school assemblies, fantasy games, comics, novels from the library, TV soaps, tabloid newspapers, many TV advertisements, some pop videos. We are realising again just how powerful, memorable and valuable stories are — and therefore how fearfully effective an influence for good or ill they can be in children's lives. They can enslave or release. So can our use of Bible stories — potentially the most powerful, memorable and valuable set of stories ever.

> The realm of fairy-story is wide and deep and high and filled with many things: all manner of beasts and birds are found there; shoreless seas and stars uncounted; beauty that is enchantment, and an ever-present peril; both joy and sorrow as sharp as swords . . . The Gospels contain . . . a story of a larger kind which embraces all the essense of fairy-stories . . . But this story has entered history. There is no tale ever told that men would rather find was true, and none which so many sceptical men have accepted as true. (From *Tree and Leaf* by J R R Tolkien.)

Bible stories, particularly the Gospels, should attract rather than repel, release rather than enslave. Steve's poor use of the story of the Feeding of the Five Thousand immediately enslaved rather then released the children in his group. It gave them guilt without hope, even though his ultimate goal was the freedom that children can find by being completely dedicated to Christ. This can't have been how it felt for them at the time! No, we must use Bible stories with children in a way that releases them.

'Everyone has sinned and is far away from God's saving presence' (Romans 3:23). This verse gives the one who loves God an opportunity to change because it is quickly followed by 'But by the free gift of God's grace all are put right with him through Christ Jesus, who sets them free' (Romans 3:24). The Bible does not speak of guilt without hope, and especially not in its stories.

Real-life stories of God at work

Real-life Bible stories aren't primarily about God's rules. Normally, they don't explicitly teach moral values, though we often give the impression that they do — as Steve did — when we use them with children. We are desperate to unpick the stories, to unravel the mystery, to dot the moral i's and cross the behavioural t's, as we pull out dubious lessons which aren't really the point of the story or which are simply not valid.

Real-life Bible stories are snapshots of God at work. Whichever story we explore, we find God doing something important in his eternal plan to save. We see him at work through the history of Israel and the rest of the world, shaping his fickle, fallible people. Perhaps most obviously, we discover his influence on and through the life of one or more individuals in spite of their failings. As we see him creatively and lovingly at work on all these levels, we shall recognise him more easily at work in our own lives, and be filled with the hope that he will work in them even more.

Use stories carefully

We think that Bible stories are easy to explore with children. And so they are, in a way: they are fairly straightforward to tell or watch on video; children like them — they can get into the stories easily and relate to the characters. However, the hard part comes when we want to explore what the stories are actually about. This is when we need to be especially careful.

Stories stay with their hearers for a very long time, and the more powerfully they are told, the longer they stay. If children remember clearly the details of a real-life Bible story, if they have explored it with someone they love and respect, who has kept God in view all the time, they will gain a true impression of who God is and, implicitly, any illustrations of God's standards that the story contains. Then, in the children's memory, the Holy Spirit has the story material to work with for evermore as children continually return to the stories, vulnerably and with affection, but also as a challenge to holy living.

The Bible belongs to children as well as to adults. At times we hear, 'The Bible is an adult book.' In a way this is true. Many of the realities of our faith, expressed in great doctrines of the Scripture, are beyond the grasp of young children. But God's word speaks powerfully to boys and girls as well as to adults. Truths they can understand – and experience – are embedded in Bible stories which have been told and retold for thousands of years. The stories of the Bible are a vital part of our heritage. They speak in vivid, timeless images, revealing who God is, affirming his love for us, and teaching us how to respond to him and to one another . . .

Reflecting on his own use of stories in treating children, the great psychologist Bruno Bettelheim writes in *The Uses of Enchantment* (Random House, 1975), that 'for a story to truly hold the child's attention, it must entertain him and arouse his curiosity. But to enrich his life, it must stimulate his imagination; help him to develop his intellect and to clarify his emotions; be attuned to his anxieties and aspirations; give full recognition to his difficulties, while at the same time suggesting solutions to the problems which perturb him. In short, it must at one and the same time relate to all aspects of his personality – and this without ever belittling but, on the contrary, while simultaneously promoting confidence in himself and his future.' There is no greater resource for children than the stories of the Bible. Bible stories express the human condition and probe man's inner problems, yet explore them with a hope offered by their testimony to God, who speaks through them to young and old. (From *Talkable Bible Stories* by Larry Richards.)

Bible stories point us and our children to God. They show us what happens when he met with people who got it wrong much of the time, but in and through whose lives he was at work. The stories do this by stimulating thought and imagination, stirring deep-felt emotions, encouraging solutions for our own lives, and turning them all to God. Even when Bible stories have a clear message of what doesn't please God, they point towards heavenly freedom rather then hellish imprisonment.

Story invites story

In your Bible, find and read through Luke 15:1–7, the Parable of the Lost Sheep. Notice Jesus' narrative technique:

He spots the need of the people he is with and tells his story to match it.

He uses clear biblical imagery that the Pharisees and teachers would have recognised only too well.

He draws his listeners into the story by exciting their curiosity – 'Why, in the middle of Jerusalem, to us respectable people, is he suddenly talking about the filthy, disreputable job of keeping sheep?' – and by asking them a question – 'What do you do?'

He uses as few words as possible to deliver the maximum impact, though in other instances (for example, The Good Samaritan) he uses a longer, structured story to raise the tension.

He doesn't explain away every element of the story, but makes one point about what God is like.

He invites them, with no explicit word of invitation, to tell a story of their own lives because the connections are obvious – 'This story is about a sheep being lost and found, and supposedly worthless people being lost and found. So, what is your attitude to God's idea of saving them going to be? How will you respond? God goes *looking* for the lost, not like you Pharisees who only wait for repentance.'

He looks for a response from them to what they have heard, thought and felt.

He finds other stories about people and things being lost and found, to add new dimensions and make the truth more memorable.

Bible stories are not so much 'personal' stories but stories about the formation of the people of God. However, children often *do* relate the details of Bible stories very closely to what is happening in their own lives.

> Biblical stories . . . have a way of being used by children to look inward as well as upward. It should come as no surprise that the stories of Adam and Eve, Abraham and Isaac, Noah and the Ark, Abel and Cain, Samson and Delilah, David and Goliath, get linked in the minds of millions of children to their own personal stories as they explore the nature of sexuality and regard with awe, envy or anger the power of their parents, as they wonder how solid and lasting their world is, as they struggle with brothers and sisters, as they imagine themselves as actual or potential lovers, or as actual or potential antagonists.

The stories are not mere symbolism, giving expression to what people go through emotionally. Rather, I hear children embracing religious stories because they are quite literally inspiring – exciting their minds to further thought and fantasy, and helping them become more grown, more contemplative and more sure of themselves.' (From *The Spiritual Life of Children* by Robert Coles.)

When we hear stories, they make us want to say, 'Yes, that's what it was like when I . . .', or 'That's a bit like when Aunty Carol . . .'. or 'I wish I could be like that instead of . . .', or 'I wonder what would happen if I did that. Maybe I'll give it a try . . .' We want to match story with story, including our own life story. Story invites story – this is what it is for. Bible stories help us to see God at work in the lives of others, with the result that, hopefully, we will long for him to work in ours too.

∾ Storytelling ∾

Let's begin to see how we can allow Bible stories to work in this way in the lives of children. Consider a situation in which you are not following a course, a programme or a series, but have complete freedom of choice about which Bible story to use.

• Choose a Bible story which you think may make some ready connections with the children's lives. This may be no more than a hunch at the outset, but we must allow for the guidance of the Holy Spirit as we long for real help for our children. In any case, any story is relevant!

Some stories will be difficult for children to understand and identify with. Some will clearly be stories that they grow into as they gain greater experience of life and a broader picture of the many aspects of God's nature. But just because stories are difficult or stretching doesn't mean that we should necessarily avoid them. For those children with whom we don't have frequent contact, however, we do need to be more selective and choose stories that won't leave unhelpfully disturbing thoughts or images of God or of themselves. Generally, with children who have frequent, adult Christian contact, we can safely use more of the Bible than we would instinctively be inclined to use. The choice of Bible story is wide open – we and the children will be able to sort out any difficulties or questions encountered over a period of time. What about using, then, some of those Old Testament stories that we might normally avoid for one reason or another?

• Work with a broad enough sweep of the story to give the context to the part of the story you particularly want to focus on. The story's original hearers would have known, for instance, the history and geography of the time, the images used and the allusions made. We don't. We will have to present the story in such a way as to fill in as many of these clues as possible.

• If you are retelling the story in your own words, get to know the Bible version well – the main facts, the order of events and the snippets of conversation. Write them down in summary if necessary. Prepare to tell the story with an action-packed beginning, lots of vivid description, a climax or high point, and a short, clear ending. In fact, keep the whole thing clear and coherent, without spending too long on unimportant details.

Plan to recreate part of the story – taste the food (loaves, fish, honey), visit the place (a lake, a lonely place, a crowded area, a tree by a stream) – or re-enact what happened, using the Bible text and mobilising the children as the different characters. Above all, get the children to be part of the event and to work out how the different characters might be feeling, why they were doing what they were doing, and what they might have thought God was doing at the time.

• Watch out for difficult or new words or concepts. Paraphrase them or be prepared to explain them.

• Ask yourself what was happening immediately before the story took place and immediately afterwards, and what in general God was doing with his people at the time. This will help you get an 'angle' on the story and know which parts of it to emphasise. You will need to flick backwards and forwards in your Bible to check this out.

• Introduce the story to the children by saying, in no more than two sentences, what happened before and after these events, and in general what God was doing with his people. This will give the children a framework on which to hang their understanding of what is going on in the story. It will often be possible to include this information in with telling the story itself.

• Tell the story with good use of tone, pitch and pace in your voice, and with lively facial expressions. Be your own audio-visual aid!

• Make sure you draw the children into the story all the way through, and help them to see that this story also has something to do with *their* lives. You will find an example of this in 'Plans for growth', with a re-working of the story that Steve used at the beginning of the chapter. Ask questions and make observations which let the children know implicitly that the story is about 'them then', but also about 'us now'; the big ideas contained in it were true then and are true now; the same God who is behind 'their story then' is also behind 'our story now', and he may want to work in the same ways with us. In other words, the story of the Bible goes on in our lives. But don't ask so many questions that you wreck the flow of a good story.

You may also want to include stories about your own life and experience of God, or the life and experience of other Christians you know, either contemporary or from the past. Your story will include brief 'asides' which root its big ideas into real life.

I was reading a Bible story book one evening with Lucy. Moses was on Mount Nebo just before his death. (Not the kind of story you would automatically think of reading with a child!) The story and conversation were fascinating (and slightly scary!) for both of us.

Me: *At last Moses climbed the mountain. He looked long and*

steadily at the promised land, stretching below. And there he died. No one knows where he was buried. God took care of that.
(I paused to see what she might make of that. There was a puzzled expression on her face.)
Lucy: Who looks after us when we die?
Me: Ah, well . . . There are people called undertakers who make sure we're well looked after. Yes, we don't need our bodies any more by then, so they look after them. But God looks after the bit that's not our body and we go to be with him in heaven.
L: What do they do with our bodies?
Me: Well, you remember on Sunday when we walked through the churchyard. Those huge stones mark the places where people's bodies are buried in the ground.
L: Will I be put in the ground one day?
Me: Yes, we all will.
L: What will I be in?
Me: Perhaps a wooden box.
(Help! I was beginning to wonder how far we should go with this conversation. But then we got to what was really on her mind.)
L: Will it have my name on it?
Me: Yes.
L: Will it just have 'Lucy' on it or my full name?
Me: Oh, your full name, of course.
L: Well, everyone will know that it's me then, won't they?

Another piece of the jigsaw was put in place for her as the result of listening to a Bible story. Knowing that Christians will be with God in heaven allowed us the freedom to talk about the earthly side of death. She was beginning to see her own life story from God's perspective.

• As you come to the end of the story, if you think the children can handle it, ask our big questions about God:

Who does this part of the Bible tell us God is, directly in the words or because of the kinds of things he is doing or saying?
What is God like in this passage?
What has he done? Or what is he doing now? Or what will he do?

What does God want?
What doesn't he want?
What might it be like to live with this God?

• Ask the children, 'Do any other Bible stories tell us the same thing? Do any tell us something different about God?' This will help to build on their image of God, perhaps to add something new about him to what they know already. Then ask them what they would like to say to God in response to the story. The answer may be 'Nothing!' or there may be reflective silence or a babble of talk *about* God and then *to* him.

• Repeat stories as often as children want to hear them. Most children's stories have repetition written into them, but many Bible stories do not. Familiarity and 'comfort' will more likely come through hearing the whole story again and again.

With this light-handed approach which treats both the Bible and children with integrity, our young 'trees' will, hopefully, want to drink in the never-drying 'stream' of Bible stories for the rest of their lives.

∾ Plans for Growth ∾

Plan 1
Give yourself a treat and listen to a short story or drama on the radio. As you listen, try to make as many connections between the story and your own life as possible. Draw four columns on a sheet of paper and write the following headings in each one:

> *Column 1* 'A character like me'
> *Column 2* 'A situation like me'
> *Column 3* 'A difficulty I face'
> *Column 4* 'Something I would like to become'

Then write your thoughts in these columns as you listen to the story.

On another occasion, read (or better still, have someone read to you) an episode from one of the Gospels, and do the same exercise with the columns, changing the last column to 'Something God wants to do'. At the end of the exercise, commit your response to God.

Plan 2

Here is Steve again, but this time he is using the story of The Feeding of the Five Thousand in a much more valuable way. He has chosen the story carefully and prepared it thoroughly. Underline the things that are different this time, and try to work out why they have changed.

To get things started, Steve organised a game which involved the children buzzing round the walls as fast as they could, trying to find as many different pictures as they could of things that God had made. He had cut these out from magazines beforehand and had hidden them round the room. As they arrived in twos and threes, he told them that he was challenging the whole group to find all fifty items before the session really got under way. They had to work together to put all the items they found on a table in the middle, and stop when they reached fifty.

Three minutes to go . . . two minutes . . . one minute. There was a mad dash round to find the two missing items. And there they were behind the curtains – a burger and a mountain. Phew! Just in time!

'Hello! (Hello, Steve!) First, tell me this. Have you ever been so excited about something that you forget what the time was? (Yes, when . . .)

'I certainly have. I remember the day I was twelve. I got a new bike. Straightaway, I jumped on. Dad shouted, "Don't be late for tea. It'll be in half an hour!" Well, one hour later I got back home. I'd known what the time was and that I was going to miss tea, but I was just so excited about being out on my own new bike!

'Wow! God has made lots of things for us to enjoy. He didn't actually put my bike together, but he made the metal and rubber and gave people brains to work out how to make rubber and metal into a bike.

'Just before our story starts, people were wondering who Jesus really was. Just after our story ends, they tried to make him king and maybe get him to live in a huge, posh palace. But that wasn't what Jesus wanted. No, he wanted people to see how much they

needed God. So, what on earth did Jesus do to make them want him as king? 'Are you all ready for the story, then? (Yes! No!) Good. Here we go.

'Thomas came crashing in through the front door. He was breathless. He had run all the way down from the hills. He was so excited about what had happened. He'd been with Jesus all day. Has Jesus been with you all day? What do you think? (Dunno! Yes! Not when I was in the loo! . . .)

'Thomas blurted out, "Listen, Mum. I know I should have been home an hour ago, but the most amazing thing has just happened. I've been out in the hills listening to Jesus. There were thousands of us! Like a load of sheep we were, all following him around . . . Well, I knew it was getting late, Mum – we all did – but we just didn't want to go home.

' "Wow, the way Jesus talks and the things he says – Mum, he's the best!" Thomas went on. "Anyway, we were all getting really hungry when some bloke came and tapped me on the shoulder and said, "'Ere, sonny. Give us your five loaves and two fish. The Master wants them." ' Well, what would you have done? (Smashed him in the face! Asked him what he wanted them for! Nothing!)

' "I gave the man my bread and fish," said Thomas. "Jesus took my whole lunch and . . . and somehow made enough food from it for everyone. Everyone had a bellyful! And there was tons left over too! Tons!

' "And do you know what, Mum? I suddenly had a thought. There's only one person who has ever been able to create something out of nothing before. No, it couldn't be! Jesus couldn't be . . . God, could he? I mean, I was right there with him. He was right here with us. He couldn't be, could he?'

'That's the end of today's story. So, what is Jesus like in this story? (Dunno! Nice! Kind! Amazing! Generous! God! . . .) Can you think of any other Bible stories that tell us the same thing? (Errr . . .) Do any tell us something different? (Yes, the one about . . .)

'What one question would you have liked to ask Jesus if you'd been Thomas? . . . What do you want to say to God now? . . . We'll try our hardest to be quiet for a minute . . .'

If you have a group to prepare for, or one or more of your

own children to read Bible stories with, go through all the
preparation stages above. Gradually this kind of preparation
will take less time, but it is a good discipline to make into a
habit.

If you are reading bedtime stories with your own family,
it may seem a bit 'over the top', but these times together
with your children could be made even more worthwhile
by the inclusion of some of the ideas in this chapter. Go on,
try them!

You will find a ready-made Bible story session as Bible
Activity 13 'Bible Storytelling' (page 170).

∽ Chapter Nine ∾

'I'VE GROWN OUT OF IT'

ROOT PROBLEM

'So much of the Bible doesn't seem to matter.' The child's comment said it all really. He had grown up enough, he felt, to make a critical judgement about the Bible, and he had come to the conclusion that there were parts of it that weren't important. Unfortunately, many children come to the same conclusion about the *whole* Bible.

Perhaps, inadvertently, we encourage this attitude. Well, when was the last time we heard someone in church reading from Lamentations? Or when did we ever snuggle up with our own children and Leviticus, or explore Jude in our children's groups?

And there are Bible quizzes. Ah, yes – there are some pretty hideous Bible quizzes around, like this one called 'Where are the women, then?' Surprisingly, it is all about women in the Bible!

Q: *Huldah was the wife of Shallum, a court official during the reign of King Josiah. What does her name mean – 'weasel', 'horrible smell', 'beautiful' or 'beloved of the Lord'?*
A: *Weasel.*

Q: *Once, David was insulted by a rich man called Nabal. David was really angry and took 400 soldiers to teach Nabal a lesson. What did Nabal's wife do to defuse the situation?*
A: *She set out to meet David and offered him 200 loaves of bread, two leather bags of wine, five roasted sheep, seventeen kilogrammes of roasted grain, 100 bunches of raisins and 200 cakes of dried figs. Yummy!*

Q: *What was the last thing Queen Jezebel did before she died?*
A: *She brushed her hair and put eyeshadow on. She died after being thrown from a window. Her blood spattered the wall and good*

King Jehu drove his chariot over her body. With good kings like that, who needs bad ones?

I don't like Bible quizzes much, more because of what they *don't* achieve and because of the impression they *don't* give than because they do harm. (I'm allowed to say this because the questions we have just overheard were part of a quiz that *I* put together!) Too often Bible quizzes ignore God completely, as this one seems to do. They celebrate the minute details of people's lives but omit the main point – what God was doing in and through the minute details.

'Bible Trivia' is actually a contradiction in terms and therefore not a brilliant name for a game. Every part of the Bible is significant, and shows that the Bible is about us and people like us. Even more than this, in and behind it all we can see our eternal God doing something much more important than we can imagine. The Bible brings the mundane and the divine together: God makes his people's daily lives part of his huge purposes for the whole of creation. The bigger the picture we have of God's plan, the more the minute details make sense, though of course not every detail is equally important.

In his book *Waiting* (InterVarsity Press, 1990), Ben Patterson says of suffering, 'What we see God doing is never as good as what we don't see.' The same is true of details in the Bible. Every book of the Bible is important, and so is every detail in every verse in every chapter of every book.

GROWING TREES

A baby enjoys the pieces of a jigsaw puzzle. She holds them, turns them round in her hand, bashes them together, puts them into her mouth, looks at the colours, maybe recognises a hand or a foot on them, then with a chuckle throws them away and picks up others. Jigsaws are meant for fun, and this is exactly what she's having.

With delight, a three-year-old discovers that two, three, then four jigsaw pieces fit together, to make something bigger that he recognises. He has noticed that the sticking-out parts of the pieces fit the holes on other pieces – he knows that he has to take into account what's going on around the edge. They're the same colour and shape as before, but now there is a new kind of enjoyment as the picture on the puzzle becomes much more important to him.

At five, a child easily puts all the jigsaw pieces together to create the big picture. Now all the pieces make even more sense — those she wasn't at all clear about now fit into a special place. Completing the puzzle gives immense satisfaction.

Now, I'm not suggesting that God has deliberately made the Bible as hard as possible to understand by chopping it up into small bits! He hasn't. But eventually we will need not only to help our children enjoy the individual details, characters and stories of the Bible, but also to broaden their horizons and build up the bigger picture of what God is doing throughout, and therefore to build up a better understanding of why the minute details are important.

From the time they first hear and enjoy a Bible story abbreviated, illustrated, but unexplained, children will begin to grasp the truth about God. Gradually, they will need to grasp more of it. As a result, their image of God and of themselves will continue to grow. It is important to recognise that each stage of growth will depend upon and include the preceding stages, and that the following age ranges are only a rough guide.

1 (0—4 years old)

We have already thought about the power and lasting value of enjoying all the Bible stories with children just as they stand. When these remain fixed in children's memories, the big ideas and 'God values' encapsulated in them remain fixed too. The concrete mental image of Zacchaeus scrambling down a tree to get to Jesus is a much more vivid memory for children than the truth that Jesus cares even for the 'baddies' no one else loves, and wants them to be part of God's kingdom. As long as the concrete image stays with them, the truth remains too, even though it may not be thought through and acted upon. Unless the children make the first move, there is no need to talk about all that we know is going on behind the story.

Which resources?

We will need short, retold Bible story books with many large, colourful illustrations.

What kind of help?

Times when children can 'snuggle up' trustingly with an adult to enjoy a Bible story together will be very significant. At this age, not only will their image of God be shaped by the stories they hear from the Bible but also by the *way* they hear them and by the model of what God is like which the adult provides. During this 'snuggle-up' time, any big, new thoughts that fascinate the children, which they express the desire to talk about, can be explored within the security of the relationship.

2 (5–7 years old)

We should continue to encourage children to take the sheer enjoyment of the story with them as they grow older, but now we also want to discuss with them motives, reasons, sub-plots, themes and intrigues. Our conversation will turn to what God may be doing 'behind the scenes' even though he may not actually be mentioned in every part of the story. We can begin to use our big God questions (page 00):

One golden rule about helping children to understand the Bible is never to encourage them to learn something they will need to unlearn later. We should never have to say, 'Well, actually, what you learnt when you were five wasn't exactly true. Now you're ten, I can tell you that this is what the story is *really* saying.' Our enjoyment and exploration of the story should lead children gradually into a more complex and satisfying understanding of what the story is about.

Which resources?

The books we enjoy with our children at this age will contain longer, retold Bible stories. Ideally, some of these will be the same stories they have met before in other versions, but this time seen from a different perspective and including some of the motives and reasons behind what happens. A Bible story book that goes through the whole Bible consecutively in one volume or in a series is ideal.

What kind of help?

The best kind of motivation for children of this age will still be the adult who takes time to explore the Bible story with them. In chatting about it together, the adult will hear a mixture of reality and fantasy coming from the children – parts of the Bible story mixed with ideas from other literature and beliefs and from their own imaginations. At such a time, when the child's world-view is rather a confused jumble just in the process of being shaped, adults will need constantly to refer to other Bible stories (apart from the one being explored at the time) to challenge 'strange' beliefs.

Gradually during this time, children may want to start reading Bible stories for themselves, so the books we choose must be simple enough for them to use too.

3 (8–10 years old)

Children now begin to recognise that people around the world lead different kinds of life, and to grasp some of the reasons for these differences. They will see life from the perspective of others in a simple, concrete way.

With a greater grasp of cause and effect, history and geography, there is value in setting Bible stories in their immediate context of what was going on in that part of the world at that time, and how the story leads on from what happened before it into what happened next. While, by this time, children may be very familiar with the Bible stories and less 'enchanted' by them, they may want to discover as much as they can about the facts surrounding each story.

With time, children begin to develop a sense of chronology, of events following each other in a relationship of cause and effect, or simply of events which are 'before' and 'after'. 'Yesterday' means a lot, and 'two weeks ago' has definitely not been forgotten. Their grasp of geography also grows stronger, as they realise that more places exist than just their immediate surroundings, and when they appreciate the distances involved in getting to those places.

All this will help them begin to grasp the huge expanse

of the Bible epic – the big picture of what God was doing, is doing and will do with the whole of creation. Our big questions about God will continue to play a vital role. We don't want our children to get so carried away with the facts that they miss seeing God.

Which resources?
A complete version of the Bible is a good investment for children of this age (for example, *The Ladybird Bible Story Book, The Lion Children's Bible* and the *International Children's Bible*; you might like to try a recorded version of the Bible on tape or, if you have the technology, on disk and CD Rom). A single Bible guide will introduce children to the idea of having something to help them understand the Bible.

What kind of help?
Many children will still want and need adults to explore the Bible with them, but they may also want to explore it independently. 'Casual' but frequent interest shown in what they are doing with the Bible, and encouragement to carry on doing it, will go a long way.

4 (11+ years old)
Eventually, children need help to explore in a more abstract way what the truth of the story might actually be. Part of this further exploration will be a greater appreciation of God at work behind every part of the Bible. Our big questions about God will still hold good.

However, if we continue to present only the 'single paragraphs' of God's story without showing that these are part of a 'whole book', it will be easy for children to feel they have grown out of Bible stories, out of the Bible itself, and even out of God who doesn't seem to be doing anything special either back then in history or now. Children don't have to reach this point. After all, God is infinitely greater and more awesome than anyone's brain can handle!

When a well-known story is told as a series of human events, the interest in it is exhaustible; when it is told as insights into who God is and what he is doing, it is inexhaustible. There are always new territories to explore and new possibilities to consider. What a thrilling moment when children suddenly realise that God doing something small-scale, like protecting Moses in the bulrushes, was somehow part of his vast plan 'to bring the whole universe back to himself!'

What is more, the present is actually contained within Bible history, somewhere between the epistles and the events we read about in Revelation. Children will thrill to the idea that they too can be on God's side in the big story which began before the creation of everything and goes on to a future life in the new heaven and new earth. Seeing the Bible as a whole is a powerful evangelistic tool.

Which resources?

Children will now want to discover more about the Bible and Christianity, to see if both stand up to closer scrutiny and can be trusted. A complete version of the Bible itself is vital, with a different Bible guide that will allow the possibility of children beginning to explore the biblical text by themselves, dipping into different parts of the whole story, putting the clues together and drawing their own conclusions about what is really happening in it. A Bible background book will stimulate them too, giving insights into the history, geography, culture and unity of the Bible. Versions of the Bible on computer software often have background biblical information included in the package.

What kind of help?

We will continue to explore individual Bible stories with our children if they want us to, and make clear God's involvement in the details. But we must also remind them often of the whole story – of how God creates, judges, shapes and saves his people, from start to finish. Here is a very short version of salvation history which we can use to help our children grasp the basic outline:

God created the universe out of nothing, and he made people to be his friends. But they decided to ignore him. So God chose one man, Abram, to be the start of his own special people, Israel. Gradually, God built them into a whole nation. He was their God, and he

*wanted them to obey him. But often they didn't, and they suffered
because of it.*

*Later on, Jesus lived, died and rose again so that anyone in any
country could become part of God's special people, by following him.
By the power of the Holy Spirit, Christians lived then, and still
live today, to be more like God wants them to be, until one day,
they will all be perfect, with God in heaven. Meanwhile, they
continue to spread God's kingdom throughout the world, until Jesus
returns to take them to heaven.*

Creating, judging, shaping and saving people

We have said that it is important to help our children see
the *whole* picture of God's salvation plan, because a good
grasp of this makes sense of all the details in the Bible. But
there is much more to it than that.

I have just spent two hours wrestling with a demo version
of a computer game. (It is easy to waste that amount of time
and feel as if something useful has been achieved!) In it, I
was a god who created and populated a whole world! First,
I created land, then flattened it until there was enough
farmland to support a community. The more flat land I could
create, the bigger, stronger and more populated were my
communities. Then I had to release 'walkers' who went in
search of new places to settle. The aim was for me to populate
the world with as many 'good' worshippers as possible, while
a rival god built up a following of 'bad' worshippers. Along
the way, I could influence my worshippers to find the strong-
est leaders and make them heroes, to build new dwellings,
to attack 'bad' settlements and 'bad' worshippers, 'to walk
towards each other and combine into one stronger walker'.
Finally, when the number of my worshippers was signifi-
cantly greater than the 'bad' worshippers, I could choose
Armageddon, after which only one population survived. The
end. Pretty scary stuff, but the story was complete. I had
created, shaped and (hopefully) saved my people.

Astoundingly, however, the Bible story is infinitely more
complex, more painful and more wonderful than this, and it
is full of the greatest, driving love ever – God's. People can
choose to belong to God – they are not automatons – and

the end of the 'game' isn't the end at all. There is something deeply satisfying about knowing and being involved in the whole story.

Understanding Jesus

The Bible is God's story and the story of our ancestors in the faith, which we want our children to enter into as *their* story, on God's side. It is tempting to think that all we really need to tell them are the Gospel stories, with one or two Old Testament heroes thrown in, because these are action-packed and vivid. And certainly, if I had children with me for one day who had never heard any of the Bible, I would spend the whole day telling them about Jesus as we see him in the four Gospels. He is at the very heart of our faith.

However, it is vital for us to introduce children to the rest of the Bible too. The less they know of what God is doing through the sequence of events leading up to and away from Jesus' death and resurrection, the less they will know of who Jesus himself is, and of what he did and continues to do. Outside of the Gospels, the rest of the Bible depicts graphically the reasons for Jesus' death and the consequences of it, and makes clear our own implication in what he achieved.

Consecutive reading of a biblical book forces everyone who wants to hear to put himself, or to allow himself to be found, where God has acted once and for all for the salvation of men. We become part of what once took place for our salvation. Forgetting and losing ourselves, we too pass through the Red Sea, through the desert, across the Jordon into the promised land. With Israel we fall into doubt and unbelief and through punishment and repentance experience again God's help and faithfulness. All this is no mere reverie but holy, godly reality. We are torn out of our own existence and set down in the midst of the holy history of God on earth. There God dealt with us; and there he still deals with us, our needs and our sins, in judgement and grace. It is not that God is the spectator and sharer of our present life, howsoever important that is; but rather that we are the reverent listeners and participants in God's action in the sacred story, the history of the Christ on earth. And only in so far as we are there, is God with us today also.
(From *Life Together* by Dietrich Bonhoeffer.)

> Understanding and knowing for ourselves the depths of God's love means knowing the breadth of God's word. Bible Activity 14 'Bible Panorama' (page 173) and Bible Activity 15 'Total Bible Challenge' (page 174) will help our children grasp the big story of the whole Bible.

Understanding themselves and the rest of the world

Just as the Bible story contains a beginning and an end, catastrophe, salvation, changing characters and significance in every detail, so do our individual lives. This isn't surprising since people haven't changed much since Bible times and God hasn't changed at all! The God we see at work in all creation, time and eternity is the same God who is at work in children who are Christians day by day, carrying out his vast plan. No wonder there is a deep resonance between the Bible and our own lives. It is the resonance of reality and truth. As Christian children see a beginning and an end, catastrophe and salvation, change and significance in the Bible, they will begin to trace the same in their own lives. They will know their own part in God's salvation plan, and have a deeper sense of belonging, security and purpose in him. People and their life stories come and go; the one big story carries on, with God over all.

Each human story finds meaning when it becomes part of the great story. Each of us has a role to play in the drama of salvation. Not to play it is to miss our reason for living. The key to happiness is not to do our own thing, but to find our place in God's drama. (From *Work and Worship* by Ben Patterson.)

This is the very best that we can hope and aim for as we explore the Bible with our children.

୬ **Plans for Growth** ଚ

Plan 1

Take a pile of children's story books and spend an hour quickly skimming through them. Eugene Peterson claims that five elements are present in 'all the world's stories':

A beginning and an end (an origin and a destination)
A catastrophe (the middle of a mess)
A plan of salvation (the battle and the journey)
A focus on the decisions of individual characters
Significance in every detail

How many of these elements can you find in each story book? Think carefully about how the five elements are true for the whole Bible story. Jot down the five as headings scattered round a blank sheet of paper, and have a do-it-yourself brainstorm, filling in all the concrete, biblical examples of each that you can think of.

Plan 2

Think about your own life in the context of the whole history of creation and the vast plan God has for it. What important part are you playing in it all? Try telling the story of the whole Bible story in brief, making sure that you include your own life in the part that comes before Jesus' return.

You may find you want to pray about what you have been thinking.

Chapter Ten

BIBLE EXPLORER ACTIVITIES

These activities will help you put into practice some of the thinking you have done in other chapters. This is where your exploration really starts! The activities are presented as ideas for you to use with a group of children, but they could, with a little imagination and ingenuity, work equally well with a family of one or more parents with one or more children.

Similarly, many of the activities require children to be fairly happy with reading. If this is not the case with the children you have been thinking about, start with Bible Activity 6 'Not Just Words': it offers pointers towards ways of presenting the Bible text and exploring it with children who don't read at all or very well.

1 What's the difference?

Aim: to help children see how the Bible is different from anything else they might encounter, and immeasurably more important.

Activity time: 30 minutes.

Equipment: a cookery book, some packaging (eg a cereal packet), a TV guide, a video, a tape or CD, a computer game, a poster advertising a film the children may have seen, a sports magazine, a novel, a comic, a telephone directory, a catalogue, a teen magazine, an atlas, a computer manual, a newspaper, a school text book, a translation of the Bible suitable for children.

Preparation
Think through what use each of the items listed above is to us. Prepare to talk personally, at an appropriate level, about

why you bother with the Bible and how it is different from any other source of information.

Activity

• Ask the children for suggestions about why we need the different kinds of material you have brought along. What do we get out of them? Point out the good things about each, but show their very specific, short-term use.

• Explain to the children that behind each source of information there is a group of ordinary men and women who decide what we want out of life and publish a book or magazine, or make a film, to help us get it.

• Pick up the Bible. Behind the Bible is the God who created life, the universe, every good thing that has ever existed; who knows more about everything than everyone in the world put together; who offers us this book and says, 'Here. I want you to know about me. I want you as a friend, to be close to me for ever. This book will show you how and tell you more about me. So, go on – find out more about what it says.'

• Tell your own story – why is the Bible so important to *you*? Mention the authority that these words have, which come from God himself.

2 Faith Shaper

Aim: to explore the Bible with children in a way that shapes their beliefs (with something to think about), directs their emotions (with something to feel or experience) and inspires their actions (with something to do); in other words, in a way that encourages all-round faith in children.

Activity time: 45 minutes.

Equipment: a *Good News Bible*, a torch, smoke in a jar with a lid on it, a piece of very old clothing, two or three dead flies (yes, you read it right!), some poster paints, one paintbrush for each child, a long strip of plain wallpaper, thick washable felt pens, a large sheet of paper with the heading 'What God is like and what he does'.

Preparation

In your Bible, read Isaiah 51:4–8 through carefully to yourself. It is the kind of Bible passage that we might not normally think of exploring with children.

Research the background to this part of the book of Isaiah. The Babylonians had ransacked Jerusalem, and now God's people were in captivity in Babylon. But they were not to give up hope. God would rescue them. In Isaiah chapter 51, God wants to encourage his people to leave the relative security of Babylon and set out into the unknown, back towards Jerusalem.

Read the complete 'oracle' – Isaiah 51:1–16 – for a better understanding of the verses we have focused on (vs4–8). Pray that your children will have a brilliant experience of what it means to be on the side of God the Saviour.

Now, as best you can, black out the room where you and your group will meet.

Activity

• Place a Bible somewhere in the room, open at Isaiah 51:4–8. Don't make it obvious!

• Get your group members to join together, one behind the other, to make a 'snake'. They must all remain linked. Switch off the light (as long as it is not too dark)! Then stand up somewhere high, armed with the torch. The child at the front of the 'snake' must follow the light from your torch as it leads the 'snake' round the room. Don't move it too quickly! Everyone must follow on. Take them on a course that goes round and round for a while, then shine the light on the open Bible as the end-point. Get everyone to sit down where they are. Switch on the light if necessary.

• When everyone is settled, say that God's words are like light because they show his people the right way to go, not on an actual road but in their lives. Tell them that God's people were once in captivity, but God wanted them to know that he would rescue them.

• Show the children the smoke in the jar, the piece of very old clothing and the dead flies. Make sure they know what each object is. Tell them that when they hear these things mentioned in the Bible verses you will be reading to them soon, they should point to the right object.

• Then say, 'This is what God told his people', and read Isaiah 51:4–8 as dramatically as you can, pausing slightly to open the jar of smoke at the appropriate point. Pause too at the mention of the clothing and the flies, to give the children a chance to react.

• Get the children to tell you what is wrong with the smoke, the clothing and the flies. As time goes by, smoke disappears, clothing wears out and flies die. But God said that when he rescued and saved his people, it would be for ever!

• Introduce the 'What God is like and what he does' sheet and ask one child to write on it 'Saves his people' as an example of the kind of thing they are going to write later.

• Read the Bible verses to the children again, but this time they have to listen for what God is like and what he said he would do for his people.

• At the end, ask for suggestions about what God is like and what he said he would do for his people. As a child comes up with a good answer, ask him or her to grab a pen and write/draw the answer on the big sheet, or to get a friend to do it. Some of the answers could be that God 'says' things, he 'teaches', he 'saves', he is stronger than anyone or anything ('victory'), he 'rules' and he is outside time ('deliverance . . . will last for ever').

• Display the finished sheet and ask the children how it would feel to be on the side of a God like that. God said, 'Do not be afraid . . .' (v7). Using the paints and wallpaper strip, get the children to write some of the 'feeling' words in paint, then to use the other colours to show how they would feel to be on the side of a God like that.

• When the poster is finished (and there is paint everywhere!), gather the children around it to have a look. Then try yourself to turn their expressions of colour into words of praise, making the connection that, if we are on God's side, he will keep us safe with him for ever and ever, even after the earth wears out like old clothes and the sky has disappeared like smoke.

3 Place Setter

Aim: to help a child to find his or her way round the Bible.

Activity time: 5 minutes.

Equipment: a *Good News Bible*.

No preparation is needed.

Activity

• Start with a Bible reference, for example Daniel 5:3–6.

• Find the Bible book yourself, showing the child that the name of the book appears at the top of the Bible page.

• Explain and show that the Bible book is divided into chapters (large numbers) and then verses (small numbers). Ask your child to find the start of chapter 5, then to find verse 3.

• Get the child to give you a Bible reference. He or she can pick a Bible book from the contents page and make up a chapter and verse.

• Practise this often until the child can find the verses easily. It will become clear when you can both explore the Bible's contents page together and find where the Bible book you are looking for starts.

4 Way Finder

Aim: to help a group of older children to find their way round the Bible in a fun way.

Activity time: 30 minutes.

Equipment: a *Good News Bible* for each child.

No preparation is needed.

Activity

• Open a Bible at random and gather everyone round so that they can see it. Point out the page numbers. If you have Bibles in which the numbers start again at the New Testament, show the children.

• Explain that there is an old part to the Bible (Old Testament) and a new part (New Testament), but both the old part and the new part are important. 'Testament' means agreement. By the old agreement God promised the people of Israel that he would be their God. He would love them and protect them, and he would never leave them. In return they had to obey him. Often the people of Israel did not obey him, and disaster struck. Jesus brought in the new agreement. Now people from any country in the world – not just the people of Israel – had the chance to believe and trust in Jesus, and have God as *their* God. If they did, they would have eternal life and go to be with God in heaven when they died.

• Place enough Bibles for each child in the middle of the group, but don't give them out. Get the group to work together as a team, against the clock. Tell them a page number to find, and say if it is in the Old or the New Testament. The aim of the game is for them to get all the Bibles in the room open at that page before the time is up. The confident ones will do them all to start with, and this is no problem – you don't want to make the ones who can't manage it quickly feel silly.

• Gradually reduce the amount of time you give the children to find a particular page number, and challenge them to think about working more as a team to get the job done quickly. This will hopefully involve some of the slower ones being helped by the others, but it will take the attention away from the fact that they are struggling.

• Give each child a Bible, and help them to find the contents page at the front. Show them the two Testaments again, and explain that there are many Bible books in each Testament.

Choose any Bible book and show the children how to find the page where that book starts.

● Demonstrate how to read from the bottom of one column up to the top of the next, on the same page. The text in most Bibles is printed in two columns, though most of the books that children meet in school will not be.

● Explain the division of the book into chapters and verses. Get the children to flick forwards to find the big chapter numbers and the smaller verse numbers in the same Bible book.

● At this point, return to the team race that you started earlier with the page numbers. The whole team now has to find a Bible book, chapter and verse in all the Bibles in the room, using the same rules as before. But the added rule this time is that, when all the Bibles are open at the right page, each child has to be pointing at the right verse. This may mean that some of the ringleaders in the group will show the others where to put their fingers.

● Finally, write up a few Bible references, and explain what the name and numbers mean. For the last round of the game, you could get them to race against the clock to find the verse references you have written up.

Later, you could use the same technique to introduce the children to other features of the Bible – the word list, cross references, illustrations, maps and index. Familiarity and competence with the Bible itself will be a motivating factor for helping children to carry on exploring it.

5 In Touch

Aim: to structure your Bible exploration time with children.

Equipment: a *Good News Bible*, Bible reading guides for your age group (see Resources, page 00), a Bible story book of your choice, any other equipment that will help to make the Bible verses you have chosen come alive, for example pictures or objects.

Do as much preparation as you need, and the activity can take as long as you want.

Activity

• Thank God together for the Bible and for being there to help you enjoy it and learn from it. (This helps to build up a sense of anticipation.)

• Read the Bible verses in a way that will help them come alive – aloud or silently, with great expression or through drama, using imagination or by suggesting things to look for, with pictures or symbols to focus on.

• Engage the children's thoughts, feelings and actions, so as to get 'under the skin' of what the Bible verses are about; listen to any insights that your children may have; use the Bible reading guides; make your own observations; and try to answer the big questions about God:

Who does this part of the Bible tell us God is, directly in the words or because of the kinds of things he is doing or saying?

What is God like in this passage?

What has he done? Or what is he doing now? Or what *will* he do?

What does God want?

What doesn't he want?

What might it be like to live with this God?

(This involves looking for God on every page, full involvement in discovering the truth, and learning to see our own life stories in the context of the vast epic of God's word.)

• Share together how the verses have touched you; have made you think; have enthused you to do something practical or changed your attitude; have reminded you of something else in the Bible or in your own life; have reminded you how Jesus helps to make sense of it all. (This is our response to the God we discover in the Bible, as it is expressed to each other.)

• As a result of your discoveries, pray together, responding to God in the way that you and the children find most helpful, recognising what God has said, who we are and what we are like. Try to answer the question 'So what do we want to say to God now?' (This is our response to the God we discover in the Bible, as it is expressed to *him*.)

6 Not just words

Aim: to present the Bible and explore it with children who are not so comfortable with reading.

This is not so much an activity as a set of guidelines! There are many ways of presenting Bible text to children and exploring it with them without expecting them to handle, follow or read for themselves pages of tiny, black print. These guidelines are not only good for children who struggle with reading, but also for those who can read but prefer not to because they find reading a bore.

• There are four key principles to bear in mind:

(i) We need to whet the children's appetite to engage with any biblical text, whether they hear it read aloud or they read the words for themselves. A page of text stuck under their noses will never be enough incentive for them to be excited about it. They must be convinced of the value of their struggle to follow it.

(ii) Most children can at least recognise words and probably also read them when just a small amount of printed text is placed in front of them.

(iii) Children with reading difficulties or a lack of inclination to read need as many 'hooks' into the text as possible; for instance, things to watch or listen for on the way through, or characters that they can identify with. These 'hooks' can give a sense of purpose and achievement to their struggle.

(iv) Children will always do better at following the printed text or listening to the Bible being read if there is an adult close by to focus their attention and to provide help.

• Possible ways of *presenting* the Bible text are as follows:

Sit beside a child while the text is being read aloud and point out the words on the page, inviting the child to follow them.

Sit beside a child while the text is being read aloud, and help *the child* to point out the words on the page.

Read the text aloud dramatically, while displaying (on an overhead projector acetate or a large sheet of paper) a key symbol or image from the passage for the children to focus on.

As the Bible verses are read, display the full text on acetates but with only seven or eight lines printed on each.

Display the biblical text on acetate with key words highlighted for the children to pick out.

Display the biblical text on acetate with key words highlighted so that, as you read, the children can shout these out when you come to them.

Display the biblical text on acetate with some of the key words blanked out, so that the children have to discover what is missing.

Ask the children to listen for certain things as you read the text aloud. For example, some might try to pick out some of the 'good news' in the verses they hear, while others concentrate on the 'bad news'; some might listen for all the words that describe God, while others listen for all the words that describe people.

Ask the children to make a particular physical gesture every time they hear a certain word, phrase or concept in the Bible text.

If you are reading a Bible narrative, invite the children to close their eyes (as long as the passage is not too long!) and imagine the scenes as they happen.

Learn the Bible passage by heart and recite it dramatically, maintaining eye contact with the children all the time.

Display a few simple cartoons of what is happening in the Bible verses. Don't worry – pin men still have the power to enthral, especially if they are really badly drawn!

Give the children a doodle they can draw and add to when they hear particular words or when the Bible verses mention a particular idea. Always involve the children in listening with more than just their ears!

Invite the children to 'be' one of the characters in the Bible story and to read aloud together what the character says at the appropriate points in the story. Display the whole Bible text on acetate with the character's spoken words highlighted.

Label the room to show the geography of the Bible reading, with different parts read in 'the places where they happened'. After the children have heard the story and 'seen' where it took place, challenge them to move round to the different places in the right order, retelling the story in their own words.

● Here are some hints about *exploring* the biblical text with children who struggle with reading. First, the good news! After helping them to concentrate on hearing the text being read by involving them in it as suggested above, you are more than half way towards helping them to understand what is actually going on! These pointers may help you to come up with your own ways of exploring the text.

Sit beside children who struggle with reading and help them all the way through the text.

After presenting the Bible verses, ask the children to say one thing that particularly struck or surprised them, or made them smile. Ask for any other thoughts, feelings or reactions. Accept every answer equally. If you did not have a visual focus for the presentation of the verses, ask the children what they pictured in their minds as they listened.

Chop up an enlarged version of the Bible verses into 'sense' units. If the flow of the verses is particularly hard to follow, rewrite them in your own words, in an appropriate way for your children, being careful to use a Bible commentary and any background knowledge to help you do justice to the text. Make sure that each unit is the same size and shape. Give one to each child, and challenge them to work as a team to reconstruct the verses, or the paraphrased text, within a set time.

Use Bible Activity 10 'Scribble Around'. There is nothing

wrong with using the Bible text as a huge visual aid, inviting the children to recognise words or phrases and to interact with the text in any other way they can.

Tell as many true stories as possible about the verses, to help the children see what they might mean. For example:

The story of the writer and original hearers.

The story of what God was doing with his people at the time described in this particular Bible book. How do these verses fit into the story of the whole Bible?

The story that the verses themselves tell, including the line of argument being followed, if appropriate.

The story of how you yourself have been helped by these verses.

The story of how the passage has been proved true in the life of another Christian, past or present, perhaps someone famous or in your church, or even one of the children.

Think about whether the verses could be summed up in the words of a song, in a picture, by a snappy slogan, with a series of hand or body actions, or by a combination of these. This will help the children remember the content of the Bible verses much more easily.

7 This is it!

Aim: to help children look forward with a sense of anticipation to exploring the Bible.

Activity time: 3 minutes for each child.

No equipment or preparation is needed.

Activity

• Learn this rap prayer to say with your children before you start your exploration. It is based on Psalm 119:18. Make it fun by clicking fingers, clapping, dancing . . . whatever.

Let us **see**, O **Lord**,
Show to **me**, O **Lord**.
The **amazing truths**

That are **in** your **word**.
They have **come** from **you**.
You're the **one** that's **true**.
Help me **be** and **do**
All you **want** me **to**.

• Alternatively, help your children to reflect on God as the almighty Creator, but also as the one who has something important to say to Sarah and David and Stephen and Jack and Rebecca and Timothy and . . . Use this prayer idea:

Lord, you're amazing,
You have made the sun
And the moon
And the stars
And the sea
And the mountains
And . . .

(Get the children to shout out other things to praise God for, which he has made and which we enjoy.)

Lord, you are amazing,
You made every good thing,
You can do anything you want,
You know everything about everything,
You're with everyone who loves you, wherever they are in
the world,
Yet you're here with us today and you have something
special to say to . . .

(Get the children to shout their names out one at a time.)

Lord, we're listening hard.

• Alternatively, all sit in a circle so that everyone can see everyone else. Get the children to pray aloud for the person sitting on their left. They could say the following:

Lord, please tell (name) something brilliant today.

8 Magazine Cut-up

Aim: to help children concentrate on answering the big questions about God for any Bible passage.

Activity time: 45 minutes.

Equipment: a kitchen timer or stopwatch, 5 large sheets of paper with each of the following headings on one sheet:

(1) What is God like?
(2) What has God done, or is he doing, or will he do?
(3) What does God want?
(4) What doesn't God want?
(5) What might it be like to live with this God?

For each small group of 5 children: 2 pairs of scissors, a pile of magazines and newspapers (checked through first for possible distractions!), a pot of paper paste, 2 paste spreaders.

Preparation

Get to know the context and background to the Bible verses that you have chosen to explore with your children. This will include:

Reading several chapters of the same Bible book around the chosen verses, or the whole Bible book if it is fairly short.
Checking in a Bible handbook for the aim of the writer of the Bible book.
Getting to grips with the verses by using a Bible commentary.
Thinking through how you will handle difficult concepts and words.
Finding as many different answers to the big God questions as you can.
Responding to the verses for yourself.

Pray that the children will be brought face to face with God through your Bible exploration.

Activity

• If you have a large number of children, divide them into groups of 5. If not, keep them all together and make the whole activity a challenge against the clock. Give each group a large sheet of paper with one of the big God questions written on it, 2 pairs of scissors, some paste, and a pile of magazines and newspapers. Get the children to organise themselves into 'finders', 'cutters' and 'stickers', if they can.

If yours is only a small group, have everyone work on all five sheets together as a team effort, working against the clock. Make it a challenge! But join in yourself and help them.

● Tell the children to listen to every bit of the Bible verses carefully as you read them. They are listening for answers to the big God question on their sheet of paper.

● After you have read the Bible verses, give the children two minutes only to talk together about what answers they think the verses give. (You may like to structure this part of the activity a little more carefully!)

● Then they have twenty minutes to produce a collage of whatever they have talked about by cutting words, shapes or pictures out of the magazines and newspaper, and sticking them down. The 'finders' find the words, shapes or pictures, the 'cutters' cut them out, and the 'stickers' stick them down.

● If the children have any questions about the Bible verses, they are allowed to write these down in their own words on their sheet! Encourage them to be honest about anything they are not sure of as a group.

● At the end of the time, allow the children three minutes to write on the sheet anything they wanted to say but couldn't find a word, shape or picture to match.

● Display all the collages and get each team to say anything they like about their own effort. As they do so, point out the exciting things they have discovered, correcting anything that can't be verified from somewhere else in the Bible. Avoid the temptation to answer all the questions that the children have put down; instead encourage them to ask God the questions themselves.

• Using each sheet in turn, encourage the children to make the words, pictures, and so on, into prayers of praise or thanks, or prayers for help. You could also help them to ask God the questions they have written up.

9 Life Books

Aim: to help children know that the Bible is about their real lives.

Activity time: a few minutes a day.

Equipment: a large scrapbook, a wallet-type folder or ring-binder for each child, a pot of paper paste, a spreader, felt pens, pencils, rulers, erasers.

No preparation is needed.

Activity
• Organise your children into keeping a weekly 'life book' – not a diary (though a small part of it could be a diary), but a record of their life represented by items they stick into a scrapbook, wallet-type folder or ring-binder.

Keeping a life book is more than just a Sunday, five-minute activity – the children need to make it a way of life! During the week, all the scraps that mean anything to them can be stuck into it automatically. If you are a group leader, you will probably wonder what happens to all those fun-sheets you hand out each week. Well, a life book could be the answer – they can all be stuck in there!

• Give your group members an incentive for bringing their life books to the group session each week, but do take time to look at and talk about what they have stuck in them. They don't have to do any writing especially for their life book – that would be a real turn-off. It's just a handy way of collecting some of the highlights of their life.

Some of the items that could go into life books are: tickets, brochures, programmes, drawings, church service sheets, written prayers, sweet papers, photos, birthday cards, letters, special Bible verses, discoveries about God, bookmarks, take-home funsheets, prayer requests, answers to prayer, computer print-outs, TV details, pop charts, top video charts, top computer games charts.

Most children (yes, even boys!) enjoy collecting, cutting and sticking, but the older the children, the more sophisticated the folder or file needs to be. When using this idea with 11–14s, we called the life books 'reacto-files', went down to A5 size, and had specially designed stickers for the front of them.

• A significant part of their life books will contain what the children have discovered about God from the Bible. Try to find a way of making these discoveries stand out from the rest, without putting them on separate pages. Our message is that God and the Bible are integral parts of life, not bits tacked on at the end. The divisions should be between weeks, not between the fun bits and God bits! Our real God is involved in our real lives every second of every day.

10 Scribble Around

Try 'Scribble Around' with your group or family. It's a great way to find out what they understand from some Bible verses. It's fun too, though it does assume an ability to read. We will use the story of the storm on the lake (Mark 4:35–41) as an example.

Aim: to help everyone contribute towards the understanding of a Bible passage and, with this particular part of the Bible, know Jesus better as the Son of God.

Activity time: 45 minutes.

Equipment: a long sheet of lining paper or plain wallpaper (allowing about 30 cm for each group member), Bible verses (eg Mark 4:35–41), thick felt pens or wax crayons, thin felt pens, a roll of wide sticky tape.

Preparation
Enlarge the Bible verses beforehand on a photocopier, and stick them in the middle of the lining paper. Each child will need an A4 sheet of paper with the same Bible verses on it, a thin and a thick felt pen (or a thin and a fat wax crayon).

Activity

● Set the story up by saying that sometimes Jesus' disciples must have wondered what amazing thing he was going to do next. He had just been explaining to them that God was King in a kingdom that no one could see, but that it was a real kingdom and many people would want to be the King's people. Maybe the disciples themselves were a bit puzzled by what Jesus was talking about. And how did he know so much about God anyway? Later that day, another amazing thing happened!

● Read the Bible verses dramatically, or get everyone to mime the story. Give them a fine pen or crayon and their individual sheets with the Bible verses printed on them. Invite them to do the following in turn:

Circle everything Jesus did.

In the margin, beside each action, draw a think bubble and jot down inside it (or draw a face to show) how the disciples must have been feeling at that time.

Underline any words, sentences or ideas that you don't really understand, and put a question mark against them.

Does this story remind you of any other sea stories in the Bible? Write or draw these stories in the spaces.

If you were choosing a Christian song to help us understand what this whole story is about, which would you choose? Write the name of it in a space and draw one or two musical notes beside it.

● Get the children to write words that describe Jesus around the edges of their sheets of paper, remembering what he does in these verses.

● Roll out the big sheet of paper and stick it to the floor with tape. Give everyone a thick felt pen or crayon. Ask the children to write on the big sheet exactly what they have written on their individual sheets, if they want to. If someone else has already written what they want to say, they should tick it, sign their name and make an appropriate comment. Everyone should do this at the same time, to achieve a huge creative scrum!

• When the writing and drawing have subsided, get everyone to stand round the edge of the large sheet and look at what is there. Pick out any obvious similarities or differences in what people have said. Enjoy everyone's contribution.

• Look to see if anyone's contribution is wide of the mark, and try to find a sensitive way of helping them to see why their comment may not be quite right. But look especially for any comments that help you yourself understand the story better, and highlight those.

11 Big day out

This activity is an example of the thorough and exciting exploration that your children can enjoy if you make a whole day of it. The benefits of a whole day spent together include the fun you all have, the friendships that develop, the opportunity for the leader to spend more time with his or her group, and the powerful message that comes over when an adult gives up a day for children and organises something worthwhile for them to enjoy.

Aim: to help children 'get under the skin' of a part of the Bible by using large-scale activities.

Activity time: a whole day (when you have one to spare!).

Equipment: a scroll with the Bible verses written on it, sealing wax (melted candle wax will do), a world atlas, a photograph of the ruins of Ephesus from a Bible atlas or other biblical reference book, a long sheet of lining paper or plain wallpaper (allowing about 30 cm for each group member), the Bible verses – 2 Timothy 2:3–13 – enlarged and pasted onto the middle of the lining paper, thick felt pens or wax crayons, thin felt pens, a cassette recorder with a microphone, a blank tape, a camera with film or a camcorder with tape.

Preparation

Since your group members may be experiencing hassle for following Jesus, 2 Timothy 2:3–13 would be good verses to explore with them. They are encouragement from an older Christian (Paul) to a younger one (Timothy), so this fits the situation. (This isn't the only good way to select Bible passages to use with children – God also wants to teach us things that are well outside our own experience and which don't have an obvious, immediate 'use' for us.)

First, do your own preparatory work on 2 Timothy 2:3–13. Ask yourself the big God questions about the Bible verses. Copy these verses onto a paper scroll. Make them large enough so that all the children can see them at the same time.

Organise where you are going for the day, and how you will get there. First, read through the rest of this activity so that you can decide what you want to do, and where you want to go.

Roll up your scroll and seal it with the melted wax. Hide the scroll somewhere near the front door, if you are doing these activities at home, or by the main door of the premises where you have arranged to meet.

Activity

Morning

● Use one of the 'This Is It!' activities (page 152) to encourage a sense of anticipation.

● You will have to make the children aware that these verses might have something to do with God and with their own lives. Telling the story behind the verses (the context) will 'build a window', especially if it is told in the first instance without reference to the period of history in which it takes place.

This is a true story. Once there was a young man called Tim who felt really, really miserable. You see, he was in a church where he had a very special job to do and he was a bit frightened about doing it because he was so young.

Some people were cruel and laughed at him behind his back. Some even accused him of getting it wrong about Jesus. Being shy didn't help either. Often he could only think of the right words to say long after he should have said them.

Then there was his illness. On the days when his stomach was hurting, everything seemed to be against him. He felt like giving up altogether . . . Strange really, when you think that Tim was the church leader.

• If you are planning a fun day for older children who have a sense of geography and history, fill in more of the context. Get them to go in search of a world atlas, and more precisely, a map of the Mediterranean area. (This is the start of our full involvement in discovering the truth.)

• Set your discussion in the context of any Mediterranean holidays you may have had. Point out a possible route from where you live to where Timothy lived which was in Ephesus on the east coast of Turkey. If they can use map scales, get the children to work out how far Ephesus is from where you live.

• Tell the children to close their eyes and imagine they are travelling back in time. Which events are they flying past?

• Show the photo of the ruins of Ephesus. Make it clear that we have travelled back in time about 1,930 years. But the houses wouldn't have looked like ruins – they would have been gleaming new! Ask the children to make some guesses about which houses in the picture the church might have met in. This one or that one? Maybe the Christians in Ephesus took turns to have everyone round at their house. We don't know.

• Explain that the photo shows where Tim was so miserable. But one day he received a very special letter. Someone who had been away travelling for a long, long time knocked on Tim's door and handed him a scroll. Ask the children to go to the front door to see if they can find anything.

• Before you read the scroll out, get the children to remind you why Timothy was so miserable and perhaps felt like giving up.

• Ask one small group of children or one child to listen and watch for words that suggest that sometimes following Jesus can be hard. Ask another small group or individual to listen and watch for anything that might have told Timothy that it was all worth it. Spread out the scroll on the floor and squash everyone round it so that they can follow the words as you read. Read the story with as much parent/child feeling as possible because that was the kind of relationship that Paul had with Timothy.

• Now treat this activity as a Scribble Around (page 157). Give a pen to one or two members of each smaller group and ask them to indicate on the scroll what their team members tell them are the 'suffering' words and what are the 'good news/keep going' words that might have made Timothy feel better. (Perhaps they could underline the 'suffering' words and circle those that are 'good news'.) Verses 11–13 were probably part of a well-known song that Christians used to sing. Could the group sing, shout or scribble down lines from any Christian songs that are good news for them?

• Give everyone pens and ask them to draw on the scroll anything they think is important from the verses. Look for ways in which what they have written or drawn sheds light on the meaning of the Bible passage. What they have drawn may well help you decide what you are going to do for the rest of the day!

Afternoon
• Probably most children will draw one of the images from verses 4–6, so plan the afternoon around these. You will need a cassette recorder with a microphone, and a camera loaded with film.

• Either go to a military display, if there happens to be one somewhere near, or visit the local army recruitment office; or have a go at an army assault course. Failing all these, explore a museum that has some Roman soldier displays. You could organise a treasure hunt around the museum. The final clue could be something that refers to the tough life of the Roman soldier.

Give the children the task of finding out some of the qualifications for being a soldier and some aspects of the training. Is it an easy life or a tough one? Who must soldiers obey and what are they not allowed to do? Do they ever feel like giving up? Try to get some interviews with real-life soldiers if you are at a military display.

● Alternatively, arrange a trip out to an athletic stadium or gym. Organise your own training session, but be careful in case any children are disabled or overweight. Try to talk to some athletes in training. Help the children to discover something about their training programme and also about obeying the competition rules. What are the competitors not allowed to do? In general, is the athlete's life easy or hard? Do they ever feel like giving up?

● Or you might visit a farm, preferably a working one. What is life like on a farm – easy or hard? Which times of year are especially stressful for farmers? What do they get for all their hard work? Why do they think it's worth it? Do they ever feel like giving up?

● Get the children to take photos or make a video of the soldier/athlete/farmer. Then take some photos, or make a video, of the children with the soldier/athlete/farmer, some of the children on their own and some of you all together as a group. Dash off (or send another leader or parent) to get the film processed within the hour, if you need to and it is possible.

Evening
● The main task of the evening will be to help the children identify with the soldier/athlete/farmer, and then begin relating all they have learnt to their own tough situations at school. (This is learning to see our own life story in the context of the vast epic of God's word, and our response to the God we discover there.)

First, ask the children to act out sketches to show some of the things they have learned about the life of the soldier/athlete/farmer. Be quite clear about the point of the sketch each time. Soldiers are required to obey their commanding officer and to do what they have been chosen and trained to do. When on duty, they don't do the things that ordinary civilians do. Athletes have to keep the rules both when they are in training and when they are in the race or competition. Both the training and the event itself are tough – there are no short-cuts, and cheating only gets them disqualified. Farmers work hard, and farming is not always easy. If farmers want to be paid and to enjoy what they have worked for, they must be prepared to put in the time and effort beforehand.

● Watch the sketches and remark on any new insights into the Bible verses that they give us.

● Show the photos or video of the soldier/athlete/farmer. Say that the Bible verses aren't really about soldier/athlete/farmer – they are about Timothy and ourselves, following Jesus and sometimes finding it hard. Show the rest of the photos or video of individual children and the group, and have a laugh!

● Ask the children the big God questions in relation to these Bible verses, and discuss their answers:

What is God like?
What has God done, or is he doing, or will he do?
What does God want?
What doesn't God want?
What might it be like to live with this God?

● Ask the children if they have any questions they would like to ask God about all this.

● Allow time for children to pray silently, if they want to. Ask the following questions, encouraging them to turn their answers into prayers:

What do you find hardest about following Jesus?
Why do you think it's worth following Jesus? (Remember the Bible verses.)
Who or what helps you to keep going?
If you could say a one-sentence, very honest prayer about keeping going as Jesus' follower, what would it be? (One sentence only, beginning 'Lord . . .')

● So far it has all been a bit tame, so let's liven things up a bit. Give a felt pen to each child and as many paper plates as you can afford! Have lots of reels of sticky tape available. Ask the children to write on their paper plates one thing or person or fact that helps them want to keep going with Jesus (or they can draw pictures of these things). Now give yourselves a time-limit of ten minutes to construct an appropriate model of the soldier/athlete/farmer out of all the paper plates, as a reminder of the day.

• The day after your session, use the list of explorer's skills again (see page 00), to check how many of them your fun day included. Was there a good mix of thinking, feeling and doing activities? If not, arrange another Bible fun day soon and try to adjust the balance!

12 Gotta get a message to you

Aim: to explore different kinds of writing from the Bible in ways that 'unlock' the text appropriately for children.

Activities

Stories and histories
• Produce a photo-story or video with the children playing all the characters.

• Ask the children to retell the whole Bible story as a rap or other rhythmical poem.

• Compile a local newspaper, with children playing the parts of reporters, photographers, editors, printers, distributors – all in one or two session!

• Do a role-play or scripted drama.

• Map out the floor into numbered areas where each 'scene' of the Bible story takes place, and walk round improvising the scenes.

• Create a storyboard for a forthcoming film of the story.

• Mime the Bible story in teams, with each team forming and holding a pose that illustrates a 'scene' from the story; the other team must guess what is happening.

• Read out the Bible story as you go round a venue which

is similar to where the action takes place, for example a cathedral for the Temple, or a church/synagogue for the synagogue.

Laws

• Invent stories of what people did that might have led God to invent a particular law.

• Guess which laws are actually in the Bible. Find some obscure laws and mix them with others you have made up. Ask the children to guess which are the real laws and which are not, and to say why they think so. Ask them why God would or wouldn't make a law like that. This will help them to discover more about what God is like.

• Fill in the cultural background to the laws you are exploring, then get the children to act out 'courtroom dramas' that tell the story of the breaking of one of these laws and show the possible consequences of breaking it.

• Stick Old Testament laws on separate pieces of card and place them round the room. Ask the children to go round all the cards and answer the question 'What did God care about back then?' Gather everyone together, check their answers and ask 'What does God care about now?' Use some of Jesus' teachings and some New Testament letters to help the discussion.

Proverbs and wisdom

• Beforehand, make up three or four letters arising out of the problems that the letter-writer has encountered by going against the advice offered in a proverb you have chosen. Get children to read them and think of some possible solutions.

• Invite the children to draw a humorous cartoon to illustrate a proverb of their choice.

• Make a video diary entitled 'A day in the life of . . .', which follows the story of a child's day from morning to night but inventing realistic situations that illustrate proverbs from a particular chapter.

• Ask children to write their own proverbs addressed to

well-known TV personalities or pop stars, basing them on God's values.

Poetry and songs
• Play some games using a parachute, which recreate the changing moods of a psalm; big, violent actions for stormy emotions; small, gentle actions for calm moods.

• Enjoy making a huge, painted banner representing the mood of a psalm, with just one or two of the psalm's words depicted and using colour without pictures to form an abstract portrayal.

• Ask children to write their own poems in the same vein as the Bible verses, but with words they themselves want to say to God in response.

• Use clay, plasticine or playdough to shape moods or images used in the poetry.

• Have fun with a keyboard to create a backing track that suits the mood and sense of the poetry.

Prophecy
• Use a complete 'oracle' (ie verses that are grouped together under a single heading in your Bible) or a meaningful amount of prophecy. Avoid using just one or two verses.

• Read the verses out loud and record the prophecy on tape, focusing the children's attention on pictures or actual examples of the images that the prophet uses.

• Have the big God questions written up on sheets of paper and hung about the room so that they are always in mind. Don't be afraid of having a straight discussion to find the answers to them.

Gospel episode
• For accounts of things that Jesus did, use the same methods outlined in 'Stories and histories'.

• Ask the children to act out the scene as if they were the crowd watching what Jesus did and hearing what he said. As they do this, the group could walk round the whole house or church, using a different room or space for each scene. Label each room/space as you go, to remind you where the scene takes place, what happens there, and how the crowd reacts to what Jesus says or does.

• Jesus came to reveal God to us, so a good question to ask the children at the end is 'What is God like, judging by what Jesus says or does in the Bible verses we have just looked at?'

• Let the Gospel episode help the children to imagine what it would be like to meet Jesus. His actions are always invitations for us to meet him, and his words are invitations for us to know what God wants for us and how to live his way. Gospel episodes always reveal God to us and say to us, 'Come and meet him.'

Letter/Epistle

• Tell the story of the church or the individual to whom the Bible letter was written. Make the story as vivid as you can. Who was the letter written to and why? What did he/she/they need that meant a letter had to be written? What was the occasion? Get this information from *The Bible from Scratch* (Simon Jenkins, Lion Publishing) or *The Lion Handbook to the Bible*.

• Read through the whole letter yourself.

• Show the children the letter in the Bible, but say that it doesn't look much like a letter we would get today. Rewrite all or part of the biblical letter on a scroll from the first century or as a present–day letter. But only do this after your own careful study of the letter. Be sure to find the link between the situation of the person or church who received it and a situation in the children's own lives. As you rewrite, use phrases that will ring bells for the children who are listening.

• Arrange for a 'postman' to deliver this letter. Ask one or more of the children to open it and read out what the letter says.

• When they have heard it, ask them is there is anything in it that they think is any of their business.

• Ask them to think about what they would like to say to God in response to what they have just heard. They could write their responses as a letter or, if you have access to a tape recorder, each child could record his or her response as if it were one side of a telephone conversation. When they have all finished, play back the recorded conversations for them all to hear.

Visionary/Apocalyptic writing
• Visionary writing is not the most obvious thing to tackle with children, but, because they *are* children, they usually have many of the skills necessary for begining to see what the writer is getting at. There is no reason why we should prevent children exploring part of the Bible just because they can't understand it *all*, as long as we don't give them a wrong impression of what it might mean. A good way to get on the right track is first to tell the story of the people to whom the vision was addressed, depicting their situation as vividly as possible.

• Pick out any images that the writer uses and get the children to look at them in picture form – in their imaginations, on a video or from your own visual aids. Ask as many questions as you can about the image used, to help the children see as many aspects of it as they can. Let's take a shepherd, for example. Does he live an easy life? What skills does he have? How much do you think he cares about his sheep? Would he be prepared to do anything risky for the sake of his sheep, do you think?

• Using the image to help you, if it is appropriate, invite the children to imagine what the difference would be for those hearing the vision between the kind of situation you have described and the kind of life God really wants for them.

13 Bible Storytelling

It can be very effective to tell a Bible story in a way that helps children put themselves in the position of one of its characters. The 'moral' of the story becomes much more immediate and the good news easier to know.

This activity tells the story behind Psalm 23. It introduces the necessary Bible background as part of the story, and makes the psalm as personal as it is in the Bible. There is nothing worse than telling a story and then giving the background details, the teaching, the 'moral' and the 'appeal' afterwards. The result is one dead story and one switched-off bunch of children!

Aim: to help children relate to the good news in Psalm 23 and be encouraged to grow in their faith in God.

Activity time: 15 minutes.

Equipment: the verses of Psalm 23 (from the *Good News Bible*) written out on a large sheet of paper or overhead transparency, thick felt pens or overhead projector pens, an overhead projector (if needed), a cuddly woolly toy lamb.

Preparation

Do all the background work thoroughly – the context, the aims of the storyteller, the original audience, the explicit or implicit teaching, and so on. We must only retell Bible stories after doing a lot of preparatory work which will probably never be noticed when we present the story. Because story is a powerful medium, our retold version must get as close to the function of the Bible version as possible. Stories always come across better if they are learnt by heart!

Activity

• Do one of the 'This Is It!' activities to help the children anticipate hearing something special from God.

• Display the words of Psalm 23. As indicated in the story outline below, highlight or circle the words from the psalm when you come to the appropriate part of the story. Do silly things with the toy lamb to demonstrate the story, but not when you reach the serious bits!

● Explain the psalm in the following way:

This psalm (displayed) begins 'The Lord is my shepherd'. That makes me and you his sheep. I don't know if you've noticed, but I'm not really a sheep. I know it's hard to believe! You see, a psalm is a poem, and in poems we often use picture language to describe things. Here the picture language about a shepherd and his sheep helps us to understand what it's like to live with God.

Then proceed to tell the story. To ensure that the children are keeping up with the action, ask them to repeat any word they hear you say which has the sound 'Baaa' in it.

Life was hard for a shepherd in those days, and pretty tough for a sheep too! You had to grow all that wool for a start — it wasn't easy! Your sheepy name is Baaa-rbara. (Baaa-rbara!) Or perhaps it's Baaa-sil. (Baaa-sil!) Or it could be Wool-liam. Anyway. You're one of the whole flock that belongs to the village of Baaa-thlehem. (Baaa-thlehem!). There's only one shepherd for the whole lot of you. Baaar-baric! (Baaa-baric!)

Well, it's spring. The winter rains are over, so there's loads of lovely fresh grass. Mmmmm! Luxury! So off you toddle behind your shepherd. He's called Baaa-rry. (Baaa-rry!) You only go a little way, then get your head down for a full stomach of nice, green din-dins. (Mark the words 'green grass' in the psalm.)

A few months later, no more fresh, green grass, but no worries! The grain has now been reaped, probably baaa-rley. (Baaa-rley!) So off you toddle a little further behind Baaa-rry (Baaa-rry!). Out you go into the fields to feed on anything that's left. Down goes your head again.

A few weeks later, no more stuff in the fields to eat, so off you toddle again behind Baaa-rry (Baaa-rry!) — a lot further this time to find some dry, sun-scorched, yellow grass. And phew! You're so tired. (Mark the word 'rest' in the psalm.) Aaah! That's better. (Mime chewing.) Mmmm . . . just like Shredded Wheat, Baaa-rbaric! (Baaa-baric!) The green stuff's definitely the best. This dry stuff sticks in your throat. You need a drink.

(Mark 'quiet pools of water' in the psalm.) Quiet pools of fresh water are the thing. Luxury! But wait a minute! There's no fresh water here. So off you toddle behind Baaa-rry (Baaa-rry!)

to a well. Here, now there are some other blokes coming up. They're helping Baaa-rry (Baaa-rry!) heave off the big stone that's over the well. That's to stop anyone nicking the water. Water's precious, you know! And out it pours, from the pot into the trough. Go on, get your head in. It's a baaa-rgain! (baaa-rgain!)

(Mark 'new strength' in the psalm. Lift up your hand pitifully!) *Ouch! You've baaa-shed your leg (baaa-shed it!). Your shepherd pulls you to his side. You struggle. He grips your leg, pours out some oil onto it from his sheep's horn flask. 'Wonder where he got that from!?' you think. He rubs it in. There, it feels better already. Last time you didn't feel so good, you'd drunk some bad water, remember? Your legs were all wobbly, so Baaa-rry (Baaa-rry!) picked you up, flung you round his shoulders and carried you.*

Usually you follow your shepherd. He doesn't keep prodding or shouting at you from behind. Oh yes, sometimes that stupid dog keeps baaa-rking (baar-rking!) his head off. He's making sure you keep up with Baaa-rry (Baaa-rry!) and don't get attacked by wild animals. You know Baaa-rry (Baaa-rry!) and trust him completely, wherever he leads you. Somehow he always knows the best way.

(Mark 'deepest darkness' in the psalm.) *Yes, you could be attacked in the deepest darkness by jackals, hyenas, bears or lions. You might even stumble over a cliff or down a gully. No, you're not on the dark path because you're lost. Baaa-rry (Baaa-rry!) has led you there. It's one of the 'right paths'.* (Mark 'right paths' in the psalm.) *Odd that, isn't it?*

You don't have to be afraid thought. Baaa-rry's (Baaa-rry's!) 'rod and staff' will protect you. (Mark 'rod and staff' in the psalm.) *His rod's about a metre long. He wears it on his belt. It's got bits of sharp stone or nails driven into the end of it. Ouch! I wouldn't like to be the bear that got a smack in the teeth with that!*

And his staff's about two metres long. A lot of the time he uses it to help him walk over rough ground or to tap you gently into place. If you get trapped in a dangerous spot, he'll hook you out with it too!

Horrible things can happen to you in the deepest darkness, but you needn't be afraid. Baaa-rry (Baaa-rry!) is with you, with his rod and staff. He'll guide you to food and water and rest. He'll heal your wounds and sickness. He'll protect you from being lost or from being snatched away from him. What more does a sheep need?

•Encourage the children to thank God silently for being their shepherd. Read the psalm all together out loud.

14 Bible Panorama

Aim: to help children see that the Bible is one whole story.

Activity time: 60 minutes.

Equipment: plenty of newspaper, a roll of lining paper or plain wallpaper, poster paints, water pots, mopping-up clothes, one paintbrush for each child, some Bible reference books showing the outline of salvation history and where different Bible characters fit in.

Preparation
Make sure you have a clear idea of the outline of the Bible story. Find a Bible handbook that has a helpful diagram of all the characters your children might have heard of. Have this to hand during the activity itself.

Activity
• Spread plenty of newspaper on the floor area. Place on top of it the largest strip of paper you can find. A roll of wall lining paper would be ideal.

• Have enough poster paints available for the number of children doing this activity. Give them one paintbrush each.

• At one end of the paper, enjoy painting a scene together to represent creation – the earth, sea, sky, flowers, animals, birds, mountains, trees, and so on.

• At the other end of the paper, discuss and then paint what you think a new heaven and a new earth might be like.

• Somewhere towards the 'new heaven and new earth' end, paint together a scene to represent life today.

• Gather the children at the 'creation' end of the paper. Walk them up to the other end, helping them to appreciate that time is passing. You could say, for instance, 'This is how God made everything in the beginning. This is what life is like today. One day, there'll be a new heaven and new earth where everyone who has ever loved God will live.'

• Get the children to sit down round the edge of the paper. Ask them to name any Bible characters they can think of.

• Using the paper as a time-line, write the name of each suggested character in pencil at approximately their point in history. Explain to the children what you are doing as you do it. Say something like, 'First came A. Years later, there was B who . . . C did the same kind of thing when . . . because God . . .' In other words, fill in an outline of the Bible story through time, showing how God's plan is working out.

If you are not sure where a character fits, check your Bible handbook or, better still, get some of the children to do it.

• All the children paint the characters they have suggested at the appropriate point on the paper.

• Ask the children to paint themselves around the scene depicting life today. Explain that they too can be part of the story that the Bible tells, and, if they love God, they are heading for heaven.

• Use the picture in any other way you can. For instance, find a way of showing some of the Bible's big themes, like creation, salvation and judgement.

15 Total Bible challenge

Aim: to help children see that the Bible is one whole story.

Activity time: 60 minutes.

Equipment: a set of Bible event cards (see below).

Preparation
Write each of the follow paragraphs on a separate card. They appear here in the correct chronological order.
God creates the universe.
People choose to disobey God and are separated from him.
God tells Abram to leave his home town of Ur and go to the land that God will show him.

Abram obeys.

Abram arrives in Canaan, the promised land.

God changes Abram's name to Abraham, meaning 'father of many nations'.

God promises to bless Abraham and his family, and to bless all nations *through* Abraham.

Abraham's son, Isaac, lives in Canaan as a shepherd.

Abraham's grandson, Jacob, lives in Canaan with his twelve sons.

Famine hits Canaan. There is not enough food for Jacob's large family.

Jacob's family moves to Egypt where one of the sons, Joseph, has become prime minister, and is in charge of the corn supplies.

Jacob's descendants live in Egypt for four hundred years. They become slaves to the Egyptians.

God makes the descendants of Jacob into a nation, the people of Israel. 'Israel' is another name for Jacob.

God sends Moses to get his people out of Egypt.

God gives them the Ten Commandments and other rules for living. Now they really are his people.

The people of Israel enter into an agreement (covenant) with God. He will be their God and they will be his people. He will love and protect them. They must obey him.

The Israelites cross the River Jordan and enter Canaan, their promised land.

Hostile tribes in Canaan try to get rid of the Israelites.

The Israelites settle in Canaan.

They have 'judges' to help them fight against the tribes that are already in Canaan. Most judges are soldiers.

The last judge is Samuel. He is not a soldier. He is a prophet, someone who tells the people what God wants them to know.

The people say they want a king, but Samuel reminds them that God is their king, so they don't need any other.

God lets the Israelites have a king – Saul. There are good kings like David and Solomon, and bad kings.

Solomon's son, Rehoboam, is a harsh king. Only two tribes

of Israelites want him as king. The other ten ask for Jeroboam, one of Solomon's generals.

Israel splits in two. The northern half of the country is now called Israel. The southern half is called Judah.

The Assyrians attack Israel and take the people captive.

The Babylonians attack Judah and take the people captive.

The Persians release God's people from Babylonia. Many return to Jerusalem in Judah. They wait for God's chosen king.

Jesus is born to save people from the wrong that separates them from God.

Jesus teaches and heals, telling and showing people the good news of God's kingdom.

Jesus dies.

God raises Jesus from death. The good news of Jesus is for everyone.

Jesus returns to heaven.

God sends the Holy Spirit to help Jesus' followers.

Saul, a Pharisee, hunts down Jesus' followers and throws them in prison.

Saul becomes a follower of Jesus and is called Paul instead.

Paul travels three times round the Mediterranean lands with the good news about Jesus.

More and more people trust Jesus. But the Romans make life hard for Christians and kill some of them.

Today, the number of God's people is still growing.

One day Jesus will return.

God will make a new heaven and a new earth, and all his people will be with him in heaven, as close to him as they can possibly be.

Activity

• With a child or group of children, turn all the cards face down. Each person in turn picks up a card.

• When he or see sees what is written on it, everyone attempts to work out, or find out, if the event happened before or after other cards that have already been placed. The first to happen ('God creates the universe . . .') needs to be towards one end of the room and the last one ('new heaven and new earth') towards the other end.

• The idea is to get all the cards in the right order through discussion and research, and then to turn them all over and try to do it without help.

• The final stage might be to try to do it against the clock, within, say, eight minutes.

∽ Chapter Eleven ∽

BUT WILL THEY GO ON GROWING?

Willow. Water-loving tree. Unsuitable for growing near buildings. All willows are hardy, quick-growing, decorative and avid for moisture . . . Plant October-February in moist soil and in a sunny position. Large trees do best near a pool. Do not plant near foundations or drains. (From *Your Gardening Questions Answered*, by Reader's Digest.)

Willow. The willow tree thrives in the damp soil of river banks and the shores of lakes. Its long, penetrating roots help strengthen the bank. (From *The Dorling Kindersley Children's Illustrated Encyclopaedia.*)

WHAT THE PSALMIST SAW

Perhaps the psalmist had willows in mind when he wrote of those who 'find joy in obeying the Law of the Lord, and . . . study it day and night':

> They are like trees that grow beside a stream,
> that bear fruit at the right time,
> and whose leaves do not dry up.
> (*Psalm 1:3.*)

There were and are plenty of willows in Israel, very distinctive with their lush, swaying foliage. Often they stand by streams, growing imperceptibly but strongly. Not only do they drink in the stream's water but, nourished by it, they develop shoots, buds, leaves, twigs and branches – beautiful new life. There is absolutely no danger of them ever shrivelling up during times of drought, because their roots reach down into the water.

We need to see Bible images like this in our mind's eye and allow them the space and freedom to 'speak' to us. Well, what do you see when you imagine a tree by a stream and think of children whose lives are firmly rooted in the Bible? Is there anything in the image that we have so far missed?

In my imagination, I always end up seeing the tree's roots stretching down into the water, and find myself asking the same question as before: How can the word of God, the Bible, be the ever-present source of life to our children, to the same extent that it was and is in the lives of children brought up in the Jewish faith? How can we help God's word to be there always for them to draw nourishment from?

GROWING TREES

Every gardening book tells us that, no matter how strong a plant is, careful attention to the conditions in which it grows is vital. Neglect of these conditions will cause a plant's premature death. I hope this book will not only have made us think through the basic principles of exploring the Bible with children – not only 'get to grips with the gardening book' – but also will have prodded us into putting those principles into practice, into 'getting our hands dirty' by doing all we can to help provide the right conditions for spiritual growth in our children as they explore God's word.

This growth comes from God, and is never quick and easy. We would probably treat with more than a hint of suspicion any commercial grower who tried to sell us a 'wonder tree' that would reach full maturity overnight! But we can help to provide the best conditions that will encourage growth into maturity long-term.

> **Bible exploration with children**
> A sense of anticipation
> Looking for God on every page
> Full involvement in discovering the truth
> Learning to see their own life-story as part of the vast
>   epic of God's word
> Response to the God they discover there

I am sure that God, who began this good work in you, will carry it on until it is finished on the Day of Christ Jesus . . .

I pray that your love will keep on growing more and more, together with true knowledge and perfect judgement, so that

you will be able to choose what is best. Then you will be free
from all impurity and blame on the Day of Christ. Your lives
will be filled with the truly good qualities which only Jesus
Christ can produce, for the glory and praise of God.
(*Philippians 1:6,9–11.*)

We are looking for our children to become 'free from all
impurity and blame'. If they trust in Christ, God will definitely keep them growing until 'the Day of Christ Jesus'
when they will be perfect, when he takes them to be with
him after his return. Until then, their outward lives will
match more and more closely the inner reality of the holiness
attributed to them through Christ's death. This is the growth
we hope for.

This is a pretty breath-taking prospect, because somehow
it is easier to imagine children left 'unnourished' by God's
word or 'unpruned', shaped only by the prevailing 'winds'
of secular values, and growing less and less perfect and blame-
less. But, as Christian children regularly 'drink in' and
respond to God's word, their 'love *will* keep on growing
more and more' (my italics). This is what we are praying for
– young plants budding, shooting, bearing blossom, growing
sturdier, then yielding fruit.

Essentially, of course, as in ourselves and other adults, we
are looking for our children to sprout the fruit of the Spirit
– love, joy, peace, patience, kindness, goodness, faithfulness,
humility and self-control (Galatians 5:22–23). This is the
most complete kind of love that anyone can have – love for
God, for other people and for themselves.

However, Paul also mentions 'true knowledge' and 'perfect judgement' as two signs of growth. For our children as
well as for us, 'true knowledge' means grasping the truth
about God and about what it means to trust him with
everything. As they respond to what they know about him,
they come to know him better as their Friend and Lord, and
to love him more and more. 'True knowledge' is not just
'knowing about' – it's 'knowing'. When children talk naturally about God, excitedly explore the truth about him
with searching questions, and clearly enjoy having him as

their Lord and very best Friend, we can be sure that they are growing in 'true knowledge'.

'True knowledge' of God and his ways needs 'perfect judgement' if it is to make any difference at all to the way our children live. 'Perfect judgement', which should follow logically from 'true knowledge', means knowing what pleases God and what doesn't, what is right and what is wrong, what is important and what is not. For children, it may not be a 'logical', rational response at all; they may never stop to think, 'If God is like *this*, I must live like *this*!' But 'perfect judgement' is a personal 'yes' to God and his ways which, consciously or subconsciously, change our children through what they discover in the Bible. Enabled by the Holy Spirit, they gradually learn to live in the very best way, day by day.

THE STREAM THAT IS ALWAYS FLOWING

To help create the right conditions for growth of 'more love', 'true knowledge' and 'perfect judgement', we must enable God's word always to be available to our children, and them always to be available to God through his word, in ways that are as continually appropriate to them as possible. We can aim for this on at least four timescales – year by year, week by week, day by day, and moment by moment.

Year by year

In chapter nine we thought about the changing needs of children when they come to the Bible, and what these changing needs might mean in terms of the resources we provide and the kind of help we give them. Children can grow out of certain Bible story books, Bible reading guides and even versions of the complete Bible, and it is only right that they should. God created them as people who grow and develop, and who consequently have different needs, enthusiasms and preferred ways of learning at different times of their lives. This is no less true when they come to the Bible. We can plan for this natural growth by thinking carefully each year what kind of help with the Bible might be most appropriate for them. As they grow up, their horizons will broaden, and this should be reflected in what we give them or do with them as we help them to explore the Bible.

Year on year, we may not always need to change the type of help we offer. Christmas and birthdays could mark a new 'era' with the Bible, when we celebrate with our children another year of listening to God and offer them the next appropriate sort of help as a present – amongst other presents!

It is vital to keep our children coming back to the same parts of the Bible time and again, so that they gain fresh insights from the same stories or Bible verses. There is always more to discover, and God always has something new to say through familiar parts of the Bible; the sooner we can help children get used to listening for these new insights, the better. It is a basic expectation which can help to ensure they never feel they are growing out of the Bible.

Week by week

Many of the Bible activities described so far, particularly those in chapter ten, would make good, once-a-week, special events – fun, frequent, stretching, and significant. What is learnt and experienced of God will help keep children going with the Bible when their individual motivation may be lacking.

Day by day

The daily (or at least regular) 'habit' of Bible exploration is an attempt to make God's word, the nourishing 'stream', available often enough for it to make a lasting impact on our lives. We are human and need to be reminded of God and his ways frequently. Many have found regular Bible reading refreshing and exactly the kind of discipline they need. Others have suggested that the daily 'habit' is legalistic, so instead they only open their Bibles when others do it with them in a group or in church, or when they have time, or when they believe God is guiding them to. They are right to claim that the Bible doesn't say anywhere that we must read it every day.

However, if exploring the Bible becomes an enthralling, vital communication between God and our children, there is no reason why they shouldn't want to read it daily, or even two, three or four times a day! Often, the more we say they *must* do it because it is the right thing to do, the more they probably won't want to. Children's own motivation is worth immeasurably more than any amount of bribery, threat, gentle persuasion or instilled discipline. If they know the Bible is a good and vital experience because it brings them face to face with God, they will be there – once a day and even more, if they possibly can!

Bible reading guides can lead them into this kind of joyful expedition through God's word. The Bible does have in it the underlying assumption that people who love God will want to hear what he has to say to them as often as possible.

If you are thinking that all this sounds less than realistic and nothing like the children you know, you are right – it is idealistic, but it is a target to aim for. Children may not easily appreciate the connection between the passionate love they feel for God and the time they spend exploring a book, so we shall need to work hard at making them want to explore the Bible daily. Here is one possible way of encouraging children to read the Bible on their own, if they have the ability:

1 Within a 'challenge time' of one week, encourage the children to read just one small section of the Bible, or one Bible story, or one day's Bible reading note and verses.

2 When one week has gone by, ask how they got on. If they haven't managed to do it, try to find out why. Offer to do it with them there and then, in case there are practical difficulties to overcome. Then issue the same challenge again for the following week.

3 As soon as the children have achieved one exploration of the Bible, the key motivational factor to do it again, or to do even more, will be to reflect with them on the following:

What was so good about what they read? What answers did they discover to our big God questions.
What did you and they believe God had to say to them through the Bible exploration?
What difference has it made, or could it make, to their lives

if they took that particular truth on board? Make sure that you tell them what you have discovered from your own exploration of the Bible during the same week.

4 Challenge the children to explore two parts of the Bible during the following week – then three, four, and so on, until you feel they have just about reached their capacity or the exercise has begun to lose its attraction. There is no harm done in giving it a rest for a short period.

Moment by moment (or at least hour by hour!)

As children continue to explore the Bible over the years, it will shape their beliefs, direct their emotions and inspire their actions – like the stream always flowing past, nourishing the tree through its roots. The tree doesn't think, 'Oh, I must suck this wet stuff up' – it just does it!

So the shaping, directing and inspiring of our children's lives won't necessarily happen simply because they systematically remember a Bible verse or story, think through its relevance to their own lives and ask God to help them change in the light of it. This will demand a lot of abstract thought and reflective self-analysis which many children cannot manage. Children tend to live first and think later. The lives of those with whom they have explored their Bibles, and occasionally the actions of characters in Bible stories, along with their lasting image of the God they have met there and their daily relationship with him, will probably have a far greater, subconscious influence on them than their conscious determination to live differently.

However, getting our children to recall Bible verses, themes and stories as ways of deliberately keeping God's word fresh and available to them, can help them to keep hold of the store of information and the vivid image of God by which they will live. First, we will have explored a part of the Bible in some depth with them, and then we will want them to remember, for as long as possible, something they have discovered.

One or more of the following ways may suit the children you are thinking of:

Memorising Bible verses

However entertaining we make it, learning key Bible verses is hard for children. Remembering them a day later is excruciatingly difficult; dredging them up two days later pretty well impossible. So we can either practise saying the verses and put them back into context so often that they become firmly fixed in our children's minds, or we must be content that they will only be remembered for a day at most. Both permanently and temporarily remembered Bible verses can be valuable.

Whichever approach we adopt, we must not only put remembered verses back into their original context often, but also make clear by our own use of them which situations they help us with. Children will soon catch on if we learn and use memory verses appropriately ourselves.

Exploring the same few Bible verses on several occasions, but always reading them from the Bible again, may mean that our children can eventually recite them word for word.

Slogans and chants

Verses may stick in the mind better when shouted as a slogan or chanted to a rhythm. Alternatively, if you have explored a longer part of the Bible together, the key truths can be summarised as a chant. This one attempts to encapsulate the gist of Psalm 145:

Praise God the King —
King of all creation,
King over the nations,
King of our salvation!
Praise God the King!
Everyone must know it,
So our lives have got to show it.
And God's kingdom?
He will grow it.
Praise God the King!

This one summarises 1 Peter 2:4–10:

We're God's temple built together,
Chosen, holy, priests Forever.

Verses written on cards
Those of us who have brains like sieves may prefer to jot
down a key verse or thought on a small card, again after
exploring the part of the Bible which sets it in context. The
card can then be put into a school bag, spectacle case, hand-
bag or pocket, so that it will fall out at us often during the
day!

Symbols, images or pictures
Instead of learning or writing down a key verse or thought,
some will find it much more helpful to put it down in
picture form. We often invite children to draw a picture of
the key event or idea in the Bible, because they are more
likely to think in pictures and stories than in abstract concepts
or disembodied words. A small card could hold the simplest
picture or symbol, but have the most profound connotations
for children when they come across it again during the day.

If this idea catches on, children could put each day's image
on a different, dated page of a notebook, and have a totally
visual record of all God has said to them. When they look
back, this may make much more sense to them than any
number of carefully copied-out verses.

Actions
Instead of a drawn picture, an image created with, say, a
hand action, may convey enough about the verse or idea for
it to make its mark on the day. Actions are fun too, particularly when you and the children struggle together to find
the best one to communicate the content of the verse.

SEEING THE TREES GROW
It will be a struggle at times to encourage this continuous
discovery and growth in our children: we won't be able to
give enough time to preparing an exciting time with the
Bible (though bringing 'excitement' to the event is always
God's prerogative anyway!); our children will get bored and
maybe even refuse to explore it any more; they will learn
and *say* one biblical thing in their prayers then *do* something
awful that goes right against it; and all the ideas we have
considered together in this book will seem to have come to

nothing. We may be tempted to throw up our hands and say, 'Well, I tried!' If some or all of this corresponds with a less than stunning experience of the Bible for ourselves, that will seal it for us: we were trying to be too ambitious; we had too high an expectation of what our children might get out of the Bible; we were only kidding ourselves if we thought that the Bible could ever be anything other than dutiful, sheer hard work for them. Then something happens out of the blue . . .

Today I've been amazed. I shouldn't have been because I've recently made a special effort to notice the tiny details in people and situations – to try to see things through God's eyes. (So my 'amazing thing' didn't amaze him in the slightest. He'd been carefully working at it for a long time.)

I don't know how many times we have read and enjoyed, with our five-year-old daughter, Lucy, the story of the paralysed man who was let down through the roof by his friends. We have seen it in picture form when I have retold the episode. We have read it in simple story books. We have seen it on video. We have looked at it in the Bible itself. Lucy's questions about it have ranged from what the roof was made of that his friends demolished, to what the man had wrong with him, to what he couldn't do because of his paralysis, to why he was so happy afterwards.

This evening a friend of ours was reading Lucy the same story in a story-book version. When he explained that Jesus had given the paralysed man a new life because of what the man could now do that he hadn't been able to do before, Lucy said, 'I want Jesus to give me a new life.' She had said it in such a way that it was clear she understood, not misunderstood. So they prayed.

The tree had been growing, nourished by the ever-flowing stream of the story of the paralysed man and his friends, and other parts of the Bible too. I hadn't noticed. Growth is often like that.

Later, when I went to kiss her goodnight, she was sitting up in bed beaming from ear to ear. 'Daddy, I've got a new life inside me,' she said. I could only think of one thing to reply. 'That's brilliant!' I said. And it was.

✎ RESOURCES ✐

FOR US TO LEARN FROM
Understanding children
Penny Frank, *Children and Evangelism*, Marshall Pickering, an imprint of HarperCollins Publishers Ltd (1992).

Ron Buckland, *Children and God*, Scripture Union (1988).

Francis Bridger, *Children Finding Faith*, Scripture Union (1988), OP.★

Jeff Astley (ed), *How Faith Grows*, Church House Publishing (1991).

Robert Coles, *The Spiritual Life of Children*, HarperCollins (1992).

Understanding the Bible
Leland Ryken, *How to Read the Bible as Literature*, Zondervan, US (1984).

Gordon D Fee and Douglas Stuart, *How to Read the Bible for all its Worth*, Scripture Union (2nd edition, 1994).

Andrew Reid, *Postcard from Palestine*, St Matthias Press (1989).

Jack Kuhatschek, *Taking the Guesswork Out of Applying the Bible*, InterVarsity Press (1991).

Max E Anders, *Thirty Days to Understanding the Bible*, Kingsway Publication (1990).

Bible atlases
Simon Jenkins, *Bible Map Book*, Lion Publishing (1985).

Tim Dowley, *Maps of Bible Lands*, Scripture Union (1987), OP.★

J J Bimson and J P Kane (eds), *New Bible Atlas*, InterVarsity Press (1990).

James B Pritchard (ed), *The Times Atlas of the Bible*, Times Books Limited (1987).

Bible background

David Alexander and Pat Alexander (eds), *Lion Handbook to the Bible*, Lion Publishing (1983).

Ralph Gower, *The New Manners and Customs of Bible Times*, Scripture Press (1987).

Bible overview

Graeme Goldsworthy, *According to Plan*, InterVarsity Press (1991).

Stephen Travis, *Starting with the Old Testament*, Lion Publishing (1994).

Stephen Travis, *Starting with the New Testament*, Lion Publishing (1994).

The Bible, book by book

Raymond Brown, *Bible Guide*, Marshall Pickering, an imprint of HarperCollins (1993).

Simon Jenkins, *The Bible from Scratch*, Lion Publishing (1987).

The Bible in Outline (London Bible College), Scripture Union (1985).

Frances Blankenbaker, *What the Bible is all about for Young Explorers*, Regal Books (1986).

TO HELP US TO EXPLORE THE BIBLE WITH CHILDREN

Theory, practical help and ideas

Victor Furnish, *Experiencing the Bible with Children*, Abingdon Press, US (1993).

Lawrence O Richards, *Talkable Bible Stories*, Fleming H Revell Co, US (1983, 1991).

The Bible and Children (Consultative Group on Ministry Among Children), British Council of Churches (1988).

Walter Wink, *Transforming Bible Study*, Mowbray, an imprint of Cassell (1990).

Patricia Van Ness, *Transforming Bible Study with Children*, Abingdon Press, US (1991).

Phil Moon, *Young People and the Bible*, Marshall Pickering, an imprint of HarperCollins (1993).

BIBLE READING GUIDES

Scripture Union
For information, write to Scripture Union Marketing
Department at 207–209 Queensway, Bletchley, Milton
Keynes MK2 2EB. Bible reading guides for adults – *Daily
Bread, Encounter with God, Alive to God.* (A new publi-
cation, *Closer to God*, will be available in the autumn of
1996.) Bible reading guides for children – *Let's Go!* (for
7–9s), *Check It Out!* (for 9–12s), *One Up* (for 12–14s).

Bible Reading Fellowship
For information, write to them at Peter's Way, Sandy Lane
West, Oxford OX4 5HG.

CWR (Crusade for World Revival)
For information, write to them at Waverley Abbey House,
Waverley Abbey, Farnham, Surrey GU9 8EP.

*OP – out of print, but you may be able to find a copy.